CLEAR
AND
DEFINITE
WORDS

CLEAR AND DEFINITE WORDS

Ronald G. Goetz

Foreword by
GEORGE HUNSINGER

Edited and Compiled by
REBECCA CLANCY AND LARRY MATTERA

PICKWICK *Publications* · Eugene, Oregon

CLEAR AND DEFINITE WORDS

Copyright © 2010 Rebecca Clancy. All rights reserved. Except for brief quotations in critical publications or reviews, no part of this book may be reproduced in any manner without prior written permission from the publisher. Write: Permissions, Wipf and Stock Publishers, 199 W. 8th Ave., Suite 3, Eugene, OR 97401.

Pickwick Publications
An imprint of Wipf and Stock Publishers
199 W. 8th Ave., Suite 3
Eugene, OR 97401

ISBN 13: 978-1-60608-150-1

Cataloging-in-Publication data:

Goetz, Ronald G.

   Clear and definite words / Ronald G. Goetz ; edited and compiled by Rebecca Clancy and Larry Mattera ; foreword by George Hunsinger.

   ISBN 13: 978-1-60608-150-1

   xiv + 144 p. ; 23 cm. — Includes bibliographical references.

   1. Language and languages—Religious aspects—Christianity. 2. Theology. I. Clancy, Rebecca. II. Mattera, Larry. III. Hunsinger, George. IV. Title.

BL65 .L2 G64 2010

Manufactured in the U.S.A.

Scripture quotations, unless otherwise stated, are taken from:

The NEW REVISED STANDARD VERSION, copyright 1989 by the Division of Christian Education of the National Council of Churches, U.S.A. Used by permission. All rights reserved.

Other Scripture quotations are taken from:

The REVISED STANDARD VERSION (RSV), copyright 1946 and 1952 by the Division of Christian Education of the National Council of Churches, U.S.A. Used by permission. All rights reserved.

CONTENTS

Foreword—George Hunsinger vii

Prologue xi

1 · Bultmann's Doctrine of the Cross
in Spite of Himself 1

2 · Paul Tillich and the Further Impossibility of Speaking
Non-Objectively about God 15

3 · Skepticism's Tenuous Reign 39

4 · Theology and the Language It Must Speak 58

5 · Postliberal Theology and the Camel's Nose 99

Epilogue 132

Bibliography 141

FOREWORD

I KNEW Ronald Goetz mainly through his activity in the Karl Barth Society of North America. He was a superb organizer of conferences, and he made a vital contribution over the course of many years to the Society's work. Besides his many academic contributions, he also served as an editor-at-large for *The Christian Century*, where he made Barthian concerns accessible to a wide audience of educated believers.

For nearly thirty years Goetz served as a Professor of Theology at Elmhurst College. For much of his tenure there he occupied the Niebuhr Distinguished Chair in Christian Theology and Ethics and served as the Chair of the department. At the heart of his academic career, however, was teaching. He conveyed his passion for theology with an authority and integrity that made him a mentor to generations of students. During the course of his academic career, he also served as the pastor of a church he himself had founded. His writing was largely confined to essays, articles, and reviews, most of which appeared in *The Christian Century*.

Goetz's interests, however, were not limited to his field. He was a self-taught art historian, with a particular interest in ecclesiastical architecture, which led him to travel extensively. He had a passion for jazz and served year after year as the Master of Ceremonies of Elmhurst College's yearly jazz festival. He was an accomplished chef who loved to entertain. He was a devoted family man, as well as a man whom many counted as their closest friend.

It is little surprise then, that only after his retirement was he able to find sufficient time to turn his attention to the writing of a book that addressed a theological problem that had consumed and vexed him most of his life—a doctrine of the atonement that would take comprehensive account of Charles Darwin's theory of evolution. When he died, the book was nearly complete. One of the minor tragedies of his life is that he was unable to finalize it. His thinking and writing were so uniquely personalized that whatever book may now come into being will not be the book he would and should have produced.

A search of his writings after his death uncovered an untitled draft of *Clear and Definite Words*. When it was discovered, no one among his family or colleagues recalled what it was or when he wrote it. He never sought publication for it, which is highly ironic, for it constitutes a charge to the church for forthright theological speech, and, invaluably, provides the groundwork for that charge in his demonstration of theology's need and right to reclaim its objective referent—namely, God. Having capitulated to philosophy's fruitless search for epistemological foundations, Goetz argues, theology has attempted in one way or another to proceed in avoidance of an ontological referent. Goetz insists, moreover, that the avoidance of ontology, or at least objectivity, is impossible, and that the attempt can only produce theology that is unstable or incoherent.

Goetz makes his case in conversations, some friendly, some prickly, with various theologians he deems as having contributed to the problem. Rudolf Bultmann's existentialism, Goetz contends, led him to sacrifice doctrine for faith, yet his paradoxical insistence upon a "doctrine" of the cross resulted in theological discourse altogether lacking in consistency. In the case of Paul Tillich, Tillich's pantheistic leanings led him to render all theological discourse symbolic, but it left him in a labyrinth of pan-symbolism from which he was never able to escape. Although Goetz's interventions on these themes might have been more effective if they had been more irenic, they nevertheless make forceful claims which deserve to be taken seriously.

Both Bultmann and Tillich were possessed of Christological commitments which made them in the last analysis, for Goetz, theologians struggling with philosophical predilections. Gordon Kaufman or Sallie McFague, on the other hand, theologians with negligible Christological commitments, unchecked by even that ontological vestige, were free to create theology from metaphorical scratch, which Goetz, in something of a send up, exposes as little more than subjectivism.

Even a theologian with unmistakable Christological commitments, like my friend the late William C. Placher, was not immune from Goetz's scalpel. If there are limitations to Goetz's analysis, they are perhaps most evident here. Whereas Goetz saw Placher's "soft perspectivalism" as a threat to theological objectivity, I myself do not. I would instead see Placher's position as a variation of the very viewpoint Goetz advances in this book.

Clear and Definite Words is not merely a book about theology, though it would be enough if it were. It is the kind of book that, though it never finally loses its way, manages to range beyond its subject. It is instructive, or at least provocative, in many ways—in its "thumbnail" historical review of the epistemology's quest for certainty, in its primer of the theology of Bultmann and Tillich, in its review of Thomas Aquinas' typology of theological discourse, and so on.

What distinguishes the book above all is the man behind it. Ronald Goetz is an engaging writer whose style is polemical, passionate, and at times poignant. But in the end, for good or for ill, he is a man of unabashed Christian faith. It could at least be said that the book is a defense of the faith. The discovery of *Clear and Definite Words* among Goetz's effects attests to the strange ways of providence—that what is lost may again be found and made to sound eternal verities, sometimes even in spite of itself. In this way, like everyone else, Goetz stands, as he knew, under the ironic slogan often adduced by Karl Barth: *providentia dei, confusione hominum.*

George Hunsinger

PROLOGUE

WHEN KARL Barth was doing theology—actually hazarding himself to God's glory in clear and definite words—he was received by the larger academic world, not to mention the larger intellectual world, with anything but disregard. In fact, despite Barth's primary insistence upon God's objectivity, he was attended—his many critics notwithstanding—with interest and respect. Contemporary theology would be wise to take note.

It is saddening, but not particularly surprising, that so much contemporary theology, with its excessive preoccupation with method and eager pandering to each new intellectual fad, is met with a bored and even bewildered shrug by the larger academic world. Jeffrey Stout's comment is a haunting condemnation: "It may be that academic theologians have increasingly given the impression of saying nothing atheists don't already know."[1] If, as some suspect, contemporary theology is merely a pious restatement of the atheistic biases of academia, then Stout's remark is justified on the face of it. If, on the other hand, it is not merely atheism garbed in an amorphous awareness of cosmic mystery, then one might suggest that in order for it to gain, if not respect, at least a certain credibility in the academic world, theologians ought to begin to take risks again—that is, risk speaking in clear and definite words about the ontological intent of their God-talk.

If theology is merely a phenomenological description of the experience of faith, if its ontological status is merely solipsism, then it is to some extent insulated by its very idiosyncratically individualistic character from all sustained secular attack. But

---

1. Stout, *Ethics After Babel*, 164.

what it gains in invulnerability it loses in relevance to humanity's concern for the truth of things. It has become clear that a theology which is vague and equivocal about its ultimate object commands, not the respect of the academic world, but only its contempt.

Indeed, while I often find myself a half-hearted, half-hoping believer who needs to hear all the arguments for faith that theology can muster, any attempt to speak about God, Jesus Christ, and the Holy Spirit in terms that avoid an ontological commitment to their objectivity simply confirms my doubts. I cannot claim to speak for all, but when I come to suspect that a given theology, in seeking to make Christianity "relevant" to the world, dissolves its traditional ontological truth claims in a soothing bath of noetic vagueness, my faith is not fortified. Instead, I want to give up on the whole business. I do not believe that I am alone in this. I cannot help believing that there are many Christians who hold their faith far more ontologically than many theologians would permit. Theologically, Christians are starved by the froth fed them by the theological left; yet they cannot, and should not, swallow the anachronistic obscurantisms pushed on them by the theological right.

Moreover, despite the strenuous efforts of contemporary theologians, it is patently impossible to do theology without an ontological agenda. Every theologian has certain ontologically held beliefs as to what is finally objectively true and objectively false; that is, what in the Christian tradition corresponds to reality and what does not. Therefore, the ontological question, the question of one's objective intent, lurks behind every theological utterance. A refusal to come to terms with the ontological character of one's assumptions is no indication that it does not exist. A failure to expound specific doctrines does not mean that hidden doctrines are not at work.

For example, one may not be a Trinitarian, but this does not mean one can avoid taking an objective stand on the question that Trinitarianism attempted to answer, i.e., How do we Christians understand the central Christian claim that "in Christ, God was reconciling the world to himself"?[2] If Trinitarianism is

---

2. 2 Cor 5:19.

wrong, then something else must be more appropriate: Modalism? Adoptionism? Arianism? Was Christ a prophet? A great man? A charlatan or a madman? The victim of the misunderstanding of the apostles? The options are limited. Every possible Christian and anti-Christian reading of the Christian claim was well known by the end of the second century of the common era, and every interpretation then and now implies a willingness to affirm what one believes is in fact the case.

Christianity does not begin in doctrines. It begins with God's self-revelation in history and humanity's corollary experience of that self-revelation. But since human beings are rational and cannot but attempt to understand and expound their experiences, Christianity is inescapably theological, inescapably doctrinal, and inescapably concerned with the objective truth of things. To attempt to avoid or equivocate on the question of the cash value of one's theological utterances inevitably brings one at best to a certain theological incoherence. Who better to demonstrate this at the outset of this tract but Rudolf Bultmann and Paul Tillich, for if theologians of this magnitude cannot avoid theological incoherence, how much less so all the lesser pates in their wake?

1

Bultmann's Doctrine of the Cross in Spite of Himself

WRITING JUST before Karl Barth tossed his existentialist hand grenade into the playground of the theologians in his 1919 *Römerbrief*, J. K. Mozley claimed that behind every seemingly non-theoretical, pragmatic experience of the saving effect of the cross of Christ, there lay, in fact, "some faintest suggestion of a theory hidden."[1] Mozley insisted that "we do not reach bed-rock in preaching facts," i.e., in non-doctrinal, brute assertions that Christ's cross has saving significance.[2]

This contention would certainly have proved totally unacceptable to those theologians who, like Rudolf Bultmann, wished to push Barth's revolutionary theological existentialism to its logical conclusions. One is reminded of Bultmann's very influential claim that "Christ meets us in the preaching as one crucified and risen. He meets us in the word of preaching and nowhere else."[3] That is, authentic faith is grounded in our immediate existential response to the proclamation of Christ "crucified and risen" and not in any doctrinal explanations to which it gives rise.

Mozley anticipated the basic outlines of this Bultmannian point of view as it was expressed in the pre-existentialist language of his time. He noted that to pragmatic Christians (for "pragmatic"

---

1. Mozley, *Doctrine of the Atonement*, 203.
2. Ibid., 204.
3. Bultmann, "New Testament and Mythology," 41.

here, read "existentialist") faith arises in the hearing of the gospel preached as "fact" and experienced in power; further explanations are unnecessary.[4] However, Mozley, while expressing some sympathy for those troubled spirits who wished to go no further, would have disagreed strongly with Bultmann's dogmatic insistence that doctrine in general and the doctrine of the cross in particular constitute essentially faithless attempts to go beyond the sheer authority of the preached word. In what follows I will attempt to show that Bultmann's non-doctrinal approach to Christianity becomes particularly untenable at the point of the cross, so that even Bultmann must at last resort to doctrine—and why it is of necessity that this be so.

Bultmann's skepticism *vis-à-vis* the question of doctrine is critical due to the enormous shadow he continues to cast over contemporary theology. If indeed he operates with the "suggestion of a theory hidden" of the cross, one might legitimately wonder if he and his followers have many more hidden doctrinal assumptions stowed in the closet or whether it is ever possible to do theology without a whole catalogue of assumptions—whether hidden or overt.

Bultmann was a lifelong disciple of his early teacher Wilhelm Herrmann. More than Kierkegaard or Heidegger, Herrmann was the prime source of Bultmann's theological existentialism, a vital element of which was the reduction of all theology to the experience of faith. Herrmann's famous contention—"God reveals himself to us only in the inner transformation we experience. . . . The religious man is certain that God has spoken to him, but what he can say of the event always takes the form of a statement concerning his transformed life . . ."[5]—lies behind Bultmann's reduction of the fundamental kerygma to the drastic claim: "The word of preaching confronts us as the word of God. It is not for us to question its credentials."[6]

---

4. Mozley, *Doctrine of Atonement*, 203.
5. Quotation in Smart, *Divided Mind of Modern Theology*, 36.
6. Bultmann, "New Testament and Mythology," 41.

By his own statements, Bultmann would seem to have no patience for doctrines of the cross. For example, he speaks of the Anselmian "doctrine of the atonement" as "primitive mythology."[7] Such a claim is but a pointed application of his general contention that *any* speech about God is possible only in terms of the most extreme paradox. As Walter Schmithals has described Bultmann's perspective on the whole theological enterprise:

> Christian theology is *essentially* dialectic. . . . It speaks of God in its insight that man cannot speak of God; in this talk it takes control of God, of whom it speaks as the one who cannot be controlled; it resolves to work in the obedience of faith and at the same time with its talk departs from the existence of faith; it means to awake faith and is a demonstration of unbelief. That is its dialectic, in which it must persevere if it is not to fall into either objectification of its subject or silence.[8]

For Bultmann, revelation is not the disclosure of doctrines of God, or mysteries about God, or anything of the sort. Rather it is "man" who is revealed. For Bultmann, in the kerygma, "*Everything has been revealed, insofar as man's eyes are opened concerning his own existence and he is once again able to understand himself.*"[9] Thus, for Bultmann, to try to penetrate in a doctrinal, objectifying way the ground out of which the existential experience of faith arises, that is, to get behind the preached word wherein Christ is proclaimed, by faith unto faith, is to distort both Christ and faith.

> To go behind the Christ who is preached is to misunderstand the preaching; it is only in the word, as the one who is preached, that he encounters us, that the love of God encounters us in him. . . . Therefore, *faith* also, like the word, is revelation because it is only real in this occurrence and otherwise is nothing.[10]

Theology is said to be sin, but silence about God and God's act in Jesus Christ could also be said to be sin. Therefore as a good

---

7. Ibid., 7.
8. Schmithals, *Introduction to the Theology of Rudolf Bultmann*, 45.
9. Bultmann, *Existence and Faith*, 85. Emphasis in original.
10. Ibid., 87.

Lutheran who at least in this respect is buoyed by Luther's *pecca fortiter* ("sin boldly"), Bultmann proceeds, yet generally within the confines of his own strict theological self-limitations—that is, in keeping with Herrmann's doctrinally agnostic stricture that theology can give expression only to the believer's own "transformed life." Thus, for Bultmann, "the theme of theology is *the man of faith*."[11]

It is difficult in the light of so straightforward an anthropocentric definition of theology's theme to refrain from observing that such language was meat and drink to thinkers like Ludwig Feuerbach, who in the nineteenth century accused theology of having "man" for its actual subject. This, according to Feuerbach, proved that Christianity at root is atheistic.[12] How readily Feuerbach would have agreed with Bultmann while drawing from such anthropocentrism an atheistic conclusion. For Feuerbach, Bultmann's very definition of theology would prove his point that it is merely "the man of faith" that is the god of humanity. Bultmann, to be sure, would have rejected such an atheistic reading of his intentions.

Clearly, Bultmann believed in God. Just as clearly, his faith in God was fundamentally anti-doctrinal in character. Insofar as he was compelled to deal with traditional doctrines, he strove mightily to find that the true subject of these doctrines was not what the naïve hearer might suppose, that is, the objective reality or doings of God. Rather, for Bultmann, no effort was to be spared to find that the real subject of those doctrines—with which even a radical existentialist could not totally dispense—was human faith. Thus, for example—and one which is in no sense isolated—of the doctrine of creation he could say,

> The primary thing about faith in creation [is] the knowledge of the nothingness of the world and of our own selves, the knowledge of our complete abandonment. . . .
>
> This knowledge does not mean to speak of God as the first cause of all beings. . . .[13]

---

11. Ibid., 93.
12. Feuerbach, *Essence of Christianity*, x–xi, 11–13, and *passim*.
13. Bultmann, *Existence and Faith*, 177.

Concerning the doctrine of the Holy Spirit, Bultmann renders such a matter as merely human activity. The Spirit is "the possibility of a new life which is opened up by faith. The Spirit does not work like a supernatural force. . . . It is the possibility of a new life which must be appropriated by a deliberate resolve."[14] Not only does Bultmann have no place for such traditional language as the Trinity or the pre-existent divinity of Christ, but programmatically, his thinking, if pushed to its logical conclusions, precludes the very possibility of such doctrines. Indeed, it would seem to preclude any doctrine which would have as its primary focus the invisible, "wholly other" God. For Bultmann, it would seem, all doctrines about God are inevitably myths, for they attempt conceptually to make the invisible God visible. In attempting to carry "the doctrine of justification by faith alone . . . to its logical conclusion in the field of epistemology," Bultmann finally contends that every prop for faith must ultimately be undercut—miracles, philosophical proofs for God, claims to infallible and historically reliable scriptures, moralism, and finally even theology itself, as theology attempts to speak about the objective reality of God.[15] Radical demythologization "destroys every false security and every false demand for it on the part of man, whether he seeks it in his good works *or in his ascertainable knowledge.*"[16] Faith is the security that abandons all security; it is to be "suspended in mid-air" after having plunged "into the inner darkness."[17]

Bultmann's theological existentialism has proved to be a highly influential statement of a general distrust, not just among many contemporary academic theologians, but even among many who regard themselves as committed Christian theologians, about the very possibility of systematic or doctrinal theology. The tendency

14. Bultmann, "New Testament and Mythology," 22.

15. Bultmann, "Bultmann Replies to His Critics," 211. I believe it was William Hamilton who once quipped that Bultmann's "affirmation" of the ancient Chalcedonian faith in Christ as the God-Man sounded more like a refutation than an endorsement.

16. Ibid. Emphasis mine.

17. Ibid.

of much modern academic theology to be all method and no substance—i.e., no actual doctrine, only endless prolegomenon—is a tendency that pushes to a *reductio ad absurdum* the existentialist horror of objectivizing theological speech. At least existentialism spoke about an urgent matter, that is, the question of faith. Much contemporary theology seems stuck at the level of the question of the question of faith.

Given Bultmann's seeming abhorrence of doctrine, it might at first glance appear surprising to find Bultmann, in the very 1942 article in which he challenged the next theological generation to embrace his demythologization program, offering nonetheless a sketchy but fundamentally complete theory, or as he preferred to call it, the "significance," of the cross.[18] However, this ought not finally to be such a shock, for Bultmann is not an atheist as some have concluded, nor a "nihilistic spellbinder" as he has seemed to others.[19] Bultmann is a believing Christian; all his negations are in the service of that which he ultimately seeks to affirm, and his affirmations are all radically tied to the cross.

To be sure, Bultmann regards the New Testament images that were used historically to undergird Western atonement theories—centering on Jesus Christ as the pre-existent, incarnate, vicarious victim who endures on our behalf the wrath of God, whose blood atones for our sins, and whose death delivers us from death—as mere "myth" or a "mixture of sacrificial and juridical analogies."[20] Obviously, Bultmann acknowledges and insists that such "myths" abound in the New Testament. Nevertheless, he contends that they fail to reflect the New Testament's actual message of the cross.

For Bultmann the cross is not myth, for the very core of the church's kerygma is grounded in "a real figure of history."[21] Thus the kerygma is "not some mysterious oracle,"[22] or a fanciful account of realities outside ourselves and our world, or the attempt to make

18. Bultmann, "New Testament and Mythology," 35–38.
19. Karl Jaspers. "Myth and Religion," 157.
20. Bultmann, "New Testament and Mythology," 35.
21. Ibid., 44.
22. Ibid.

concrete the God who is "wholly other." The kerygma points to an act of God. "God has set up the cross for us."[23]

Bultmann makes it clear that when he speaks of God acting, of God setting up the cross for us, he does not mean these words as a merely "symbolic description of a subjective experience."[24] In the face of the criticism that it is inconsistent and arbitrary for him to exempt the claim that the cross is an "act of God" from his general strictures against mythology, Bultmann insists that "if such language is to have any meaning at all it must denote an act in a real, objective sense."[25] We can know the objective truth of God's acts only in the inwardness of the existential subjectivity of faith, but that faith is nonetheless grounded in an objective act. Thus, it can be spoken of by Bultmann as having "'cosmic' importance."[26]

For Bultmann, as an act of God the cross of Christ is more than a historical event. To be sure, it is an event in history, but paradoxically it is also an eschatological event. In Bultmann's view, New Testament eschatology must, of course, be demythologized. It cannot entail a literal belief in the literal end of the world. However, interpreted existentially, the eschatological event occurs in the here and now and is an ever-present possibility to faith. By faith in the cross of Jesus Christ we are existentially crucified with him, and we literally cease to be the old persons we were, enslaved by the anxieties, cares, and lures of the world. Indeed we die with Christ to our old selves.

> The crucifying of the affections and lusts includes the overcoming of our natural dread of suffering and the perfection of our detachment from the world. Hence the willing acceptance of sufferings in which death is already at work in man means: "always bearing about in our body the dying of Jesus" and "always being delivered unto death for Jesus's sake." (2 Cor 4:10 f.)[27]

23. Ibid., 36.
24. Bultmann, "Bultmann Replies to His Critics," 196.
25. Ibid.
26. Bultmann, "New Testament and Mythology," 36.
27. Ibid., 37.

Faith in the resurrection of Christ not only completes our faith in Christ's cross, but finally the two are identical. "Indeed, *faith in the resurrection is really the same thing as faith in the saving efficacy of the cross.*"[28] There is a seeming asymmetry here. For how can faith in the resurrection and faith in the cross be one and the same if their historical basis is not? For Bultmann, the literal resurrection, the empty tomb, and so on, are mythological, while Jesus's cross is a brute fact of history. Indeed, it is its historicity that makes it a non-mythological occurrence.

Bultmann attempts to get around this asymmetry by his claim that quite obviously the *faith* of the first disciples was a historical event even if the literal resurrection was not. For Bultmann what seems to have actually "occurred" with the emergence of Easter faith was first the *apostolic existential* experience of the redemptive significance of the cross. "In this way the resurrection is not a mythological event adduced in order to prove the saving efficacy of the cross, but an article of faith just as much as the meaning of the cross itself."[29] The resurrection is the "event" for faith in which "the cross is completed."[30] Faith in the cross and in the resurrection leads to the eschatological moment in which our life in the old world quite literally comes to an end and a new world begins. By faith in the cross both we and the world are "destroyed" in the same eschatological moment. But this eschatological moment leads directly to resurrection faith. Dying with Christ by faith inevitably entails our "overcoming the natural dread of suffering and the perfection of our detachment from the world."[31] This existential transformation, being the fruit of our resurrection faith, is an eschatological event.

---

28. Ibid., 41. Emphasis in original.

29. Ibid. One must acknowledge that for Bultmann virtually everything else about the life of Jesus is in dispute. Nevertheless, in Bultmann's view, no sane historian could dispute either that Jesus lived or that he died on the cross.

30. Ibid., 42.

31. Ibid., 37.

> The "demythologized" sense of the assertion that Jesus Christ is the eschatological phenomenon that brings the world to its end is precisely this, that Christ is not merely a past phenomenon, but the ever-present Word of God, expressing not a general truth, but a concrete message, that Word that destroys and in destruction gives life.[32]

Faith achieves humanity's freedom from sin. Sin is not a myth. It is inauthentic existence. "Sin is self-assertion, self-glorying. . . ."[33] Modern "man" may well regard sin as a myth, but it ceases to be so when by faith, "the love of God meets man as a power which embraces and sustains him even in his fallen, self-assertive state. Such a love treats man as if he were other than he is. By so doing, love frees man from himself as he is."[34]

This is all God's act:

> At the very point where man can do nothing, God steps in and acts. . . .
> St Paul is endeavoring to express this when he speaks of the expiation of sin, or of "righteousness" created as a gift of God rather than as a human achievement.[35]

However, God's "gift" is the cross itself. Yet faith in that act of God, it would seem, is our responsibility. For faith is not the supernatural gift of God's Spirit.[36] Such a concept of the Spirit Bultmann brands mythological. Modern "biological man cannot see how a supernatural entity like the πνεῦμα can penetrate within the close texture of his natural powers and set to work within him. Nor can the idealist understand how the πνεῦμα working like a natural power can touch and influence his mind and spirit."[37] For Bultmann, the "Spirit" demythologized is reduced to "the possibility of a new life which is opened up by faith. The Spirit does not work like a super-

---

32. Bultmann, "Case for Demythologizing," 193.
33. Bultmann, "New Testament and Mythology," 30.
34. Ibid., 31.
35. Ibid.
36. Ibid., 26.
37. Ibid., 6.

natural force. . . ."[38] Thus there remains the critical question: "How do we come to believe in the saving efficacy of the cross?"[39]

Finally, as stated, the answer lies in the brute authority of the preached word itself. The Holy Spirit, historical arguments, pseudo-philosophical and theological proofs are rendered as presumptuous as they are useless. This is the meaning of Bultmann's claim, quoted earlier: "The word of preaching confronts us as the word of God. It is not for us to question its credentials."[40] We do not question the preached word; on the contrary, the preached word questions us as to whether we will believe or deny its eschatological claim. "It is the possibility of a new life which must be appropriated by a deliberate resolve."[41]

Seemingly, in order to bring Bultmann in line with a more immediately recognizable Lutheranism, Walter Schmithals tries to deflect Bultmann's celebration of the sheer arbitrariness of faith and the claim that we cannot question the credentials of the preached word but only appropriate it by an act of "deliberate resolve." Schmithals hopes that by putting the matter "in dogmatic terms," that is, by the device of translating Bultmann's radically existentialist claims into traditional doctrinal concepts—in this case, a full-blown doctrine of the Holy Spirit—he will to be able to make more traditional, even orthodox, sense of Bultmann's anti-orthodox stance.[42] Schmithals is correct about the tradition: traditional dogmatic theology holds that we come to believe the proclamation of the cross and resurrection of Jesus Christ by a work of the Holy Spirit. But it is absurd to suppose that Bultmann's insistence on the naked authority of the preached word can be clarified by seeing it in the light of the ancient dogma of the Holy Spirit. Since Bultmann deliberately and frequently rejects the traditional doctrine of the

---

38. Ibid., 22.
39. Ibid., 41.
40. Ibid.
41. Ibid., 22.
42. Schmithals, *Theology of Rudolf Bultmann*, 42ff.

Holy Spirit, how can it be dragged in as a tool for understanding Bultmann's anti-dogmatic existentialism?

By this dubious ploy, Schmithals, the Lutheran, never has to face the liberal, Pelagian anthropocentrism implicit in Bultmann's identification of faith with autonomous human decision. There were those on the theological left who would push Bultmann in the direction of a naturalism and even atheism (Fritz Buri, but even more so Herbert Braun), but there was also a far more "traditional" wing of Bultmann supporters, as exemplified by the Lutheran Schmithals, that tried to accommodate Bultmann to the "dogmatic" tradition by such invalid translations. However, to speak of the Holy Spirit in connection with Bultmann's theology of the preached word does violence both to traditional Lutheranism and to the integrity of Bultmann's neo-Lutheran enterprise.

In summary, for Bultmann, the "significance" of the cross—his doctrine of the cross—comes to this: God gave up Jesus to be crucified and "set up the cross for us." By our deliberate resolve to have faith in that event (which Bultmann sees as the "miraculous" act of God), we receive the "Spirit"—the Spirit being nothing supernatural but a new life opened up to us by that act of faith in which we take to ourselves Christ's death. By our existentially dying with him we are set free from both sin, i.e., self-glorification, and the anxiety of having godlessly to cling to the tangible realities of the old "dead" world. This, in turn, sets us free to commit ourselves in faith and love to others. It leads to authentic life. Having seen God's love and "self-commitment" in the cross, we now have a firm ground for "our own self-commitment."[43]

What is this but an existential restatement of the exemplarist theory of the atonement, the belief that Jesus died in order to illustrate to an alienated world the love of God? The indispensable human sequel to this act of God is that we are so moved by the spectacle of God's love so powerfully revealed in the death of Jesus in the cross that we seek reconciliation with God. *We* are alienated from God until *we* realize in the revelation of the cross

---

43. Bultmann, "New Testament and Mythology," 33.

just how much God in his love wills to do for us. Or as Bultmann puts it, in the cross we see that God's love is not a "piece of wishful thinking."[44] We are motivated to live new lives in God's love and to manifest that love to others. "We are free to give ourselves to God because God has given up himself for us."[45]

The most obvious difficulty in Bultmann's version of the exemplarist theory of the atonement is that in his work as a historian, Bultmann denies that the historical Jesus voluntarily accepted his self-sacrificing death. However, by this denial Bultmann the historian would seem to undercut Bultmann the theologian, for if Jesus was merely the unwitting pawn in God's "act," how can one find justice in God's setting up Christ's cross? Bultmann's version of the exemplarist theory does not even attempt to make sense of the question of the justice of the cross. For the older exemplarists there could be no justice if Jesus did not freely offer himself, indeed, if his acceptance of his death did not spring from his own deepest will.

Of central interest with regard to Bultmann, however, is that he constitutes an excellent example of the quite predictable difficulties inherent in any theological attempt to remain intentionally non-atheistic on the one hand, and to avoid across-the-board, objective, doctrinal language, on the other. In Bultmann's case, he could not have been theologically coherent had he consistently avoided a doctrine of the cross. Bultmann with his existential interpretation of Christian theology might not seem to "need" many Christian doctrines. However, he does require the cross. His own faith experience compelled him to affirm the centrality of the cross and thus it compelled him to say concretely what he thought it all meant.

Since Bultmann is not a Trinitarian, denying as he does the Holy Spirit and the pre-existence of Christ, he is able to achieve a neat dovetailing of his own personal disdain for Nicene orthodoxy with his sweeping existentialist claims that all such doctrines are faithless, mythological attempts to make the invisible God visible. Since he takes a rather Pelagian view of human freedom, he would

44. Ibid., 32.
45. Ibid., 33.

have no need to come to terms with the sorts of problems underscored in the ancient doctrines of election or grace or the work of Holy Spirit. His doctrine of creation is essentially a confession of utter human mortality or nothingness. These examples suffice to indicate how it is that Bultmann can manage to dissolve the need for so many dogmas, doggedly insisting that we can speak only about our faith experience and eschewing all ontological statements about the ultimate source of faith.

However, in the last analysis Bultmann is not a theological solipsist; that is, he does not hold that all theology is merely a symbolic way of describing the mysterious heights and depths of our subjective feelings. Since he believes that objectively God has acted and continues to act in the cross and in the preached word about the cross, it is on the question of the cross that he must unavoidably make some genuinely objective, indeed, ontological theological affirmations—the adequacy or inadequacy of these affirmations being a further matter—but objective they inevitably must be.

Yet, even here it should be underscored that Bultmann makes such concessions only because he was forced to do so by his critics, only because he was made aware that there was no other way for him to escape solipsistic subjectivism. Still, it is no source of joy for him. He takes no delight in the privilege of speaking about the objective reality of God. On Bultmann's lips such speech was merely his almost grudging recognition of the requirements of the logic that drove him, if only at the juncture of the cross, to abandon his doctrinaire existentialism and speak about a real act of God.

It is little wonder that in the midst of unrelenting pluralistic and skeptical turmoil a Bultmannian theology of radical expressionism and existentialistic paradox speaks to many:

> When worldly happenings are viewed as a closed series, as not only scientific understanding but even workaday life requires, there is certainly no room for any act of God. But this is just the paradox of faith: it understands an ascertainable event in its context in nature and history as the act of God. Faith cannot dispense with its "nevertheless."[46]

46. Bultmann, "Case for Demythologizing," 199.

To his credit, as a Christian theologian Bultmann never compromised on this "nevertheless." Because of this, and because he rejected what Bultmann supposed a scientific worldview "requires," the existentialist philosopher Karl Jaspers bitterly accused him of doing justice neither to science, nor to philosophy, nor to theology. Indeed, according to Jaspers, Bultmann's program of demythologization constituted little more than "a most peculiar mixture of false enlightenment and high-handed orthodoxy."[47]

Bultmann had hoped that, in spite of his ultimate appeal to an almost orthodox confessionalism—i.e., that the cross was a genuine act of God—there might be a way to express his faith in terms that were sufficiently modern so that his reduction of Christianity to its essence would not give quite so blatant offense and perhaps would even gain approval by "modern man." By sufficient qualification and hedging we might stumble onto a "God-talk" which could even prove "relevant" to moderns. To some, such a tactic may have proved successful; however, for Jaspers—and he was not alone—the very attempt to win "modern man" to the faith by seeming to stand foursquare with rationalism, skepticism, existentialism, scientism, etc., yet finally holding on to the kerygmatic "nevertheless" and the doctrinal baggage that logically finally pertains to such a "nevertheless," seemed a dishonest intellectual outrage.

---

47. Jaspers, "Myth and Religion," 157, 179.

2

Paul Tillich and the Further Impossibility of Speaking Non-Objectively about God

RUDOLF BULTMANN, in attempting to meet the challenge of rationalism, skepticism, and existentialism, sought to rid theology of all myth, but finally and paradoxically maintained that the proclamation of an act of God in the cross of Jesus Christ must remain the one critical exception to his otherwise ruthless program of demythologization. Indeed, for Bultmann, the cross was the irreducible kerygma, the thing itself. The cross was a divine act in an "objective" sense.

Paul Tillich would seem to have gone even further in his apologetic strategy of trying to meet the modern scene part way. In his theological system he rendered all theological discourse "myth" or "symbol." If in his undertaking Tillich proved to be programmatically successful, he could avoid objective theological discourse altogether. Even such a bare-bones theological objectivity as Bultmann's would thus not be required.

The problem Tillich created for his own theological coherence in pursuing this goal is instructive, for it serves as another critical illustration of how difficult, indeed impossible, it is to ground one's thought in the redemptive work of Jesus Christ—or as Tillich preferred, the "New Being" as historical occurrence—and yet remain systematically equivocal *vis-à-vis* the ontological status of Christianity's truth claims. Tillich's theology is adduced here because he, like Bultmann, remains a theological giant, whose influence, at least in American theology, continues to be enormous.

Tillich and Bultmann have often been associated. Indeed, both are rooted in the nineteenth-century liberal theological tradition. Further, both were in their own ways indebted to Heideggerian existentialism. Yet it would be a mistake—an error commonly made—to assume that their views could fairly easily be made to dovetail.[1] Clearly, they did not see themselves as fundamentally allied in a common enterprise. Neither had much to say about the other. Tillich did credit Bultmann, together with Albert Schweitzer, with being his major influence *vis-à-vis* the *historical* status of the New Testament.[2] However, in his *Systematic Theology*, Tillich's main reference to Bultmann *qua* theologian finds Tillich criticizing Bultmann for his focus on the "paradox of the cross of Christ."[3] It would seem that even Bultmann's one objective event, the act of God in the cross of Christ, finally stood under Tillich's prohibition against all supernaturalistic objectification. Indeed, Tillich's insistent use of symbol and myth reads almost as if it were a turning of Bultmann's demythologization program on its head. The mythological, which for Bultmann must be systematically purged from theology so that the kerygma's objective truth can be set free from all pre-modern superstition, is for Tillich an indispensable vehicle of theological affirmation. For Tillich, the theologian, rather than being embarrassed by it, should glory in the mythological or symbolic character of all theological discourse.

Tillich radically insisted that all religious speech was and had to be in the language of myth and symbol. Any religious language that is not finally understood as mythological or symbolic is revealed to be idolatrous by its very pretense to objectivity. For Tillich, objective discourse aims at a literalness that by its very nature must claim ultimacy for itself, rather than for the "Absolute" toward which Tillich believes true symbols can only point.

---

1. See Robinson's *Honest to God* for the most celebrated, albeit abortive, example of the attempt to establish fundamental correlations between Bultmann and Tillich.

2. Tillich, *On the Boundary*, 49.

3. Tillich, *Systematic Theology*, vol. 2, 106.

Tillich distinguished between symbols and what he called mere "signs." Signs, like symbols, serve as pointers, but in an objective, literal, and non-participatory manner. For example, the word "cat" is a sign that points in a purely ostensive manner to a mammal of the feline species. "Cat" is an arbitrary, and in a sense, lifeless pointer. Any other name would do as well—a cat by any other name would scratch as deep. Symbols, on the other hand, are not mere definitions but active participants in the realities they define. "The symbol participates in the reality which is symbolized."[4] Further, they have a certain life of their own. They are born out of the human existential situation and can die or remain "dormant but capable of being reawakened."[5] Signs, on the other hand, can be arbitrarily coined and established.

Not all symbols are religious; for example, a flag, to the patriot, is more than a mere sign for a nation. Rather, it focuses and evokes a wealth of memories and loyalties to the nation, feelings of commitment that cannot be expressed in merely rational terms. Flags are stitched out of dyed cloth, but if a person dies defending the flag, he or she does not die to defend dyed and stitched cloth. It is that to which the flag points as a living, vital and participating symbol for which one is willing to die. So, too, is the case with the religious symbol. It is not merely a pointer toward that which concerns us ultimately. Indeed, any religious symbol can be a true symbol only when in a self-repudiating manner it denies its own "literal" truth: "Every religious symbol negates itself in its literal meaning, but it affirms itself in its self-transcending meaning."[6]

On a personal note, I first heard and read Tillich as a young seminary student at Harvard Divinity School in the mid-1950s. When Tillich lectured on the symbolic character of all theological discourse, he became accustomed to audience members inquiring as to the effect: "Professor Tillich, do you mean that Christianity is only symbolic?" Perhaps such a straightforward question smacked of naïveté, but as a student in Tillich's classes, I recall the urgency

4. Ibid., 9.
5. *Dynamics of Faith*, 97.
6. Tillich, *Systematic Theology*, vol. 2, 9.

in the voices of those who asked such a question. Surely the questioner was not being merely naïve in fearing that the truth claims of Christianity were being put in jeopardy by Tillich's doctrine of symbols. Nor did Tillich's typical response offer much consolation: "Never say only a symbol, for symbol is the language of ultimate concern." I remember wondering, as a theological novice, if I was hearing sophisticated evasiveness or whether my own denseness was causing me to fail to recognize a straightforward answer when I heard one. Nevertheless, I could not fully satisfy myself that I was not witnessing a theological shell game. The questioner asked whether Christianity is capable of making truth claims. Yet the answer the questioner received had to do with the inevitably symbolic character of theological language, leaving the intent of the original question so obliquely handled as to give the impression it was actually being ignored.

Only later, as I became familiar with some of the vast literature on Tillich, did I come to see that such an uncertainty over the question of Tillich's ultimate *objective* intent could not be attributed solely to lack of sophistication on the part of students. Indeed, many scholars found a cloud of systematic equivocation hanging over the entire Tillichian enterprise. In one form or another, critic after critic, implicitly or explicitly, found himself or herself bemused by the following sort of question: If the object of our ultimate concern is "God," but if even "God," together with every other theological utterance, is a symbol, and if we apply the stricture that any true symbol must negate its literal objective meaning with uncompromised consistency, then to what objective reality can the God symbol ever refer? In short: What does the God symbolized by the symbol of God symbolize?

Given Tillich's doctrine of the self-repudiating character of all true symbols, could not such questions be pressed *ad infinitum* and never be resolved? Tillich's whole theology might thus seemingly be threatened by the implication that finally it is a mere tautology; that is, it is caught in a definitional circle, and for the question of the truth claims of the Christian faith, a rather vicious circle at that. Bultmann could rescue his theology from being pushed "to the logical conclusion" that God-talk is merely "the symbolic description of a subjective experience" by making a single "objective" claim—it takes only one—to the effect that to speak of God's act in the cross is "not mythology" or a symbol. (Tillich often equated symbol and myth.)

Perhaps the issue at stake here can be made clearer by an analogy to mathematics and science. Pure mathematical systems have no practical scientific application—no empirical utility. As such they are consistent and presumably "beautiful" intellectual constructs that have no apparent function outside themselves. Though it is a truism that mathematics is the language of science, it is not true that all mathematical systems can be made to serve as the language of science, for in the case of given mathematical systems no correlation between the axioms of these systems and the characteristics of the physical, empirical world can be drawn. This is not to fault pure mathematics, any more than it would be at all viable to fault an abstract painter such as Kandinsky for creating paintings that had no direct utility to the architect in his or her design of the buildings intended to house them. Pure mathematics is its own justification.

However, unlike abstract art, to which it has a certain kinship, pure mathematics has a potential practicality. In some cases, such abstract systems can be empirically employed as scientists find empirical data that invite a correlation between the given mathematical system and newly discovered aspects of the physical world. Non-Euclidian geometries were in existence long before the enthronement of Einstein's universe in the modern world. When it became clear that Einstein's universe had certain correspondences with the basic axioms of given non-Euclidean mathematical systems that were already at hand (for example, a curved and not a straight line was the shortest distance between two points), all at once such non-Euclidean systems, which prior to Einstein seemed to have no reference outside the tautological, definitional framework of the systems themselves, could be adapted and used "objectively" to describe Einstein's newly emerging vision of the empirical world.

Pure mathematics is a perfectly valid human enterprise, irrespective of whether or not any "practical" application can ever be found for it, just as abstract painting is completely justified for its own sake even though it lacks even the potential utilitarian application of pure mathematics. However, in the case of Christian theology, the question remains, can a system that functions without reference to any reality except the reality of its own definitions have any legitimacy whatsoever? Would not a "Christian" theology that pointed only to its own manipulations of symbols be a theology of utter narcissism—lacking a reference to anything save its own world of thought and therefore rendering Jesus Christ an agent of mere linguistic self-manipulation?

One is reminded of George Santayana in his famous atheistic tribute to Roman Catholicism: "There is no God, and Mary is His mother." Though he stood outside the faith, Santayana appreciated the beauty of Roman Catholic religious symbols—even though in his estimation these symbols were fundamentally false *vis-à-vis* the objective truth of things. Such an aesthetic response to Christianity is understandable. Many Europeans find Europe's ancient churches and cathedrals and the heritage of Christian art and music to be powerful manifestations of the richness of the Christian religion—regardless of whether they are alienated from the faith or style themselves atheists. No disparagement of such a reduction of Christianity is intended. The only point here is that Christian theologians, unlike the aesthetes of religion, if their language is to make any constructive contribution to the church or to have any credibility either inside or outside it, must be men and women of faith. Faith entails far more than merely an aesthetic response to the symbols of a religion in which an aesthete cannot or does not participate.

This is not the place to review the extensive Tillich literature as it bears on the question of the objective intention of Tillich's theological language. But it ought not to be surprising that his doctrine of symbols, his abhorrence of a concept of the supernatural transcendence of God, the personhood of God, or even the existence of God, has led to wildly differing readings of his intentions.

The very fact that he can be read in flatly contradictory ways has even led some to question his intellectual honesty. Many critics see him as one who, in the last analysis, was a mainline Christian—one whose doctrine of symbols and whose distaste for language about the objectively supernatural reality of God reflect a healthy anti-idolatrous awareness that the true God infinitely transcends all our conceptions and doctrinal objectifications. Still others read him as a kind of Christian Nietzsche, an early prophet of the theology of the death of God. And then there are the less friendly critics who regard him as a less than forthcoming atheist whose equivocations and systematic ambiguity keep his real intentions hidden, perhaps even from himself.

In his book, *Paul Tillich's Dialectical Humanism*, subtitled *Unmasking the God Above God*, Leonard F. Wheat surveys a fair amount of the Tillich literature to that time. Wheat's interest in Tillich was ironic in the extreme. A non-theologian, indeed, a humanistic nontheist, Wheat was a graduate student in political science and government at Harvard University during Tillich's tenure as university professor. Wheat never heard Tillich lecture, but some of his dormitory friends were students of Tillich, and at the time Wheat was mildly scandalized to hear his friends confess considerable confusion as to what this "ultra-distinguished" scholar, the "number one Protestant theologian in this country," was actually saying. Only later, as a kind of hobby, did Wheat begin to study Tillich's work, and in growing irritation wrote his book exposing, to his own satisfaction at least, Tillich's "atheism." Wheat often expressed his incredulousness over the fact that so many theologians took Tillich seriously, although they could not remotely agree with one another as to what he was saying. He believed that Tillich's entire undertaking was an atheistic "masquerade." "One only needs to browse through the growing body of literature on Tillich to appreciate how thoroughly the theological profession has been hoodwinked."[7] Wheat wrote in advance of Hannah Tillich's

---

7. Wheat, *Tillich's Dialectical Humanism*, 267–68.

exposé of her husband's lifelong philandering.⁸ One can imagine Wheat's gloating over the fact that very few of the theologians who admired Tillich's ethics could have even wildly supposed prior to Hannah's revelations that Tillich actually saw his thought opening to such freewheeling promiscuity. One doubts that Wheat would think it particularly admirable that, judged by their silence, so few in the theological community found Tillich's promiscuity particularly relevant to his theological-ethical understanding.⁹ While I do not share Wheat's, or Sydney Hook's, or Alisdair MacIntyre's, or others' bottom-line reading of Tillich as a less than honest atheist, it is not insignificant that such figures—some of the very audience Tillich claimed to be reaching for Christianity in his apologetic reinterpretation of the faith—should finally so mock the equivocal character of his attempt to reach them on their own terms that they read him as a fellow atheist who lacked the intellectual directness to admit the truth of the matter.

When pressed on the matter, Tillich eschewed any notion that Christianity could give adequate response to the divine initiative symbolized in the central Christian claim of "Jesus Christ as the New Being" in terms of a mere subjectivism. He was concerned to avoid the implication that his theology lacked any independent objective referent, and that his system was merely a self-contained tautology, its only "truth" lying in its aesthetic power to evoke a subjective, emotive response.

Thus, in the first volume of his *Systematic Theology*, recognizing that he must make at least one non-symbolic statement so as to guarantee that his system relates to some reality beyond its own self-contained definitional framework and the "truth" value of rank subjectivism, Tillich wrote,

> The statement that God is being-itself is a non-symbolic statement. It does not point beyond itself. It means what it says directly and properly. . . .

---

8. Hannah Tillich, *From Time to Time*.

9. One exception to this seeming theological conspiracy of silence is Melvin L. Vulgamore's insightful article, "Tillich's Erotic Solution."

> However, after this has been said, nothing else can be said about God as God which is not symbolic.[10]

In the introduction of the second volume of his *Systematic Theology*, Tillich acknowledged that this statement met with various public objections. Indeed, it almost certainly must do so, as it not only contradicted his doctrine of the absolutely non-literal character of religious symbols, but also contradicted a vital aspect of his apologetic undertaking, his "method of correlation." By his "method of correlation" Tillich had hoped to end forever the struggle between philosophers and theologians.

Tillich contended that while both the philosopher and the theologian take the question of Being for their ultimate subject, their approach to Being is radically different. The philosopher asks the question of the structure of Being and does so from a posture of intellectual detachment. Unlike the philosopher, the attitude of the theologian cannot be one of personally detached intellectual neutrality. The methodology of the philosopher, Tillich believes, is akin to that of a scientist; the theologian, on the contrary,

> . . . is not detached from his object but is involved in it. He looks at his object (which transcends the character of being an object) with passion, fear, and love. This is not the *erōs* of the philosopher or his passion for objective truth; it is the love which accepts saving, and therefore personal, truth.[11]

Thus, the theologian works from within the "theological circle." He does not seek to formulate the "generally valid concepts concerning religion"; these are the subject matter of philosophers of religion and are available to all people, since all religious awareness is rooted in a "mystical a priori."[12] Rather than attempt to systematize objectively this general "mystical" awareness, the theologian commits himself or herself and "claims the universal validity of the Christian message in spite of its concrete and special character."[13]

10. Tillich, *Systematic Theology*, vol. I, 238–39.
11. Ibid., 22–23.
12. Ibid., 9.
13. Ibid., 10.

Consequently, by the device of discretely allotting all objective response to the question of Being to the philosopher and all "personal" response to the question of Being to the theologian, Tillich could assert that ultimately there can be no legitimate conflict between philosophy and theology because there is no "common basis on which to fight."

> If the theologian and the philosopher fight, they do so either on a philosophical or on a theological basis. The philosophical basis is the ontological analysis of the structure of being. If the theologian needs this analysis, either he must take it from a philosopher or he must himself become a philosopher.[14]

Tillich never made it quite clear as to how, on the basis of one's subjective evaluations, one could make "claims of the universal validity" and indeed "prove that the Christian claim also has validity from the point of view of those outside the [Christian] theological circle."[15] Nor does he make clear how a truth that attains to universality could also be, on principle, nonobjective, that is, symbolic. It would seem on the face of it to make no more sense to insist on the *universal* validity of "personal truth" than it would for me to insist on the universal truth of my subjective belief that my wife is the most lovable woman in the world.

Nevertheless, many theologians found Tillich's method of correlation and its methodological concomitant—the claim that all legitimate religious language must be non-literal—to be a helpful corrective to the "doctrinal positivism" of orthodoxy, as well as a way in which to proclaim the Christian tradition in terms of a then fashionable existentialism. Therefore, inevitably, even Tillich's friendly critics found his one non-symbolic statement—i.e., "God is being-itself"—to be flawed. It was found flawed not only because it is a flat contradiction of Tillich's own doctrine of symbols, but also because it appeared to be an objective, clearly philosophic doctrine of God, a doctrine that even had a name and a long philosophic tradition behind it: pantheism. The rules of Tillich's

14. Ibid., 15.
15. Ibid., 10, 15.

method of correlation by which theology left philosophy free to do philosophy were thus clearly violated.

In response to his critics, in his rather *ad hoc* introduction to the second volume of his *Systematic Theology*, Tillich amended his one "objective" statement about God, while hoping still to avoid falling "into a circular argument." He tacitly acknowledged that his first attempt to answer those critics who asked "whether there is a point at which a non-symbolic assertion about God must be made" had misfired. Tillich granted that the statement that "God is being itself" could not serve as the logically required non-symbolic assertion after all. He then tried a second time to offer a "non-symbolic assertion about God." In answer to his own question whether there is a point at which a non-symbolic statement about God is necessary, Tillich asserts: "There is such a point, namely, the statement that everything we say about God is symbolic."[16]

Can such a statement rescue his system from being trapped in its own tautologies? Logically, indeed, grammatically, it simply will not do. Grammatically, the subject of Tillich's clause "everything we say about God is symbolic" is not "God"; the subject is "everything." In short, it is merely Tillich's non-symbolic statement about the nonobjective status of all statements within his system, and thus it patently fails to be what he claimed for it, i.e., a way out of "a circular argument." He thus seems to remain in an utter circularity.[17]

16. Tillich, *Systematic Theology*, 2:9.

17. William L. Rowe in his *Religious Symbols and God* points out that Tillich's vacillation on this question dates from as early as 1940 when the philosopher M. K. Urban first pressed him on the issue of tautological language about God. Rowe is critical of Urban's posing of the problem and would resolve Tillich's seeming contradictions by claiming that Tillich actually intended to hold to his first non-symbolic statement, i.e., that God is being-itself. Accordingly, in Rowe's view, Tillich's later qualification that "everything we say about God is symbolic" (*Systematic Theology*, 2:9) means simply that for him being-itself or God is ineffable. Nevertheless, Rowe himself is finally somewhat exasperated and acknowledges that "there does not seem to be any clear answer to the question 'What does Tillich mean by 'God'?" (*Religious Symbols*, 42) which of course was the root question which first prompted Urban's objection to what he called Tillich's "pan symbolism."

To be sure, Tillich was aware of the gravity of his logical problem here, but ironically he attempted to resolve it in terms of high paradox. He speaks of "the boundary line at which both the symbolic and the non-symbolic coincide."[18] This allows for a statement to be both "non-symbolic and symbolic at the same time." Such an epistemological paradox or "dialectical difficulty," Tillich claims, is finally "a mirror of the human situation with respect to the divine ground of being."[19] Thus, it would seem to be finally an objective, ontologically grounded epistemological given that God-talk must exist in a kind of denotative limbo.

Such systematic equivocation is in considerable tension with another seemingly indispensable aspect of Tillich's theological undertaking, his radical insistence on the objective historical fact that there was objectively a real human life that gave rise to the New Testament picture of Jesus as the Christ. Tillich's exposition of this claim arises interestingly enough out of his attempt to come to terms with the radically skeptical, albeit remote, possibility that modern historical research might one day prove that the man Jesus of Nazareth never existed. Such a possibility confronts anyone who accepts the propriety of the historical-critical approach to Scripture. No possibility can be closed to new historical discovery, however unlikely such discoveries might seem beforehand. Therefore, Tillich is not to be faulted for trying to think through beforehand a possible response to the eventuality, however remote, of the non-historicity of the man Jesus of Nazareth. And notwithstanding the fact that the answer he gives to his question—"What if Jesus of Nazareth never lived?"—borders on the astonishing.

Tillich argues that Christianity would not be essentially affected if history were to show that Jesus never lived, since even if history got his name wrong, the New Being witnessed to in the New Testament must have lived. This claim is based on Tillich's contention that if the New Being had not appeared in history, the New Testament depiction of the New Being would not have been

---

18. Tillich, *Systematic Theology*, 2:10.
19. Ibid., 9.

possible, and thus our participation in the newness of being would not be possible.

To be sure, Tillich is not personally in doubt that the man Jesus of Nazareth lived, and that in point of historical fact it was, indeed, Jesus of Nazareth who was the New Being, as the Gospels indicate. But even had the New Testament writers chosen to tell of the appearance of the New Being in what amounts to be a series of novelettes (the four Gospels), and the character of Jesus of Nazareth was but a fictionalized version of the appearance of the actual New Being, nevertheless "there is an *analogia imaginis*, namely, an analogy between the picture and the actual personal life from which it has arisen."[20] We are thus permitted to speak of the historic reality of the appearance of the New Being irrespective of the actual historicity of the man Jesus of Nazareth.

> The problem is: Exactly what can faith guarantee? And the inevitable answer is that faith can guarantee only its own foundation, namely, the appearance of that reality which has created the faith. This reality is the New Being, who conquers existential estrangement and thereby makes faith possible. This alone faith is able to guarantee. . . . [21]

One might think at first glance that Tillich is opening the door to a concept of faith that is akin to the Rorschach ink blot test, i.e., one creates for oneself in one's response to the New Testament image of Jesus as the Christ whatever truth that exists for one from within it. In short, it is a matter of the rankest subjectivity. However, it is clear that Tillich has no wish to reduce Christology to an emotive or aesthetic response. Tillich, indeed, insists that the Christians' personal participation in Jesus Christ "guarantees" not merely the subjective validity of the experience for us in our naked subjectivity, but beyond this it guarantees an objective, historical reality. On the basis of our participation in the New Testament picture of Jesus as the New Being, we can be certain that there existed in the era of the authorship of the New Testament an actual human who was in fact the New Being.

20. Ibid., 115.
21. Ibid., 114.

Tillich distinguishes between the historical, "empirical factuality" of the specific events in the life of the New Being, which "participation" clearly cannot guarantee, and the brute fact, irrespective of our uncertainty concerning the details of his life, that the New Being actually existed. All this is grounded in the extraordinary claim that our subjective experience in response to the New Testament picture is the test which validates the objective historical reality of the appearance of the New Being.

> But the picture has this creative power, because the power of the New Being is expressed in and through it. This consideration leads to the distinction between an imaginary picture and a real picture. A picture imagined by the same contemporaries of Jesus would have expressed their untransformed existence and their quest for a New Being. But it would not have been the New Being itself. That is tested by its transforming power.[22]

Tillich, in his attempt to objectify the subjective object of faith, drew a parallel to objective philosophical argument. Just as René Descartes supposed that the experience of thinking guarantees the existence of the self that is thinking, so our participation in the New Being is a proof (presumably "tested" by itself) of the one crucial, historical, empirical fact that trivializes all mere empirical details, i.e., that the New Being walked the earth in the first part of the first century of the Christian Era. It is like the "Augustinian-Cartesian refutation of radical skepticism. That tradition pointed to the immediacy of a self-consciousness that guaranteed itself by its participation in being."[23] Once again, just as Descartes concluded that in the subjective experience of thought the *objective reality* of the self was established, so Tillich believed that the experience of the New Being established the *objective historical existence* of the New Being.

It becomes clear from all this that even Tillich, when he enters the inner sanctum of his most fundamental Christological commitments, has recourse to claims that resemble what J. K. Mozley called the "facts" of the faith. Tillich, of course, insisted that such

22. Ibid., 115.
23. Ibid., 114.

"facts" can be known only in the intimacy of subjective experience, but even the pre-existentialist Mozley would not have denied this.

Tillich's rather incredible attempt to ground the truth of the historicity of the New Being in our believing response failed to elicit much theological support. Many have found it to be, as D. Moody Smith, Jr. suggests, a bit of theological "sleight of hand."[24] Nonetheless, no matter how excruciating its logic, the argument remains significant, for its very implausibility underscores Tillich's theological dilemma. Since he is and wishes to remain a Christian, Tillich is compelled to resort to such extraordinary devices in order to rescue his Christology from the decidedly solipsistic bias of his philosophy of religion. Tillich fully understood that Christianity is grounded in a concrete, historical occurrence. Yet the question remains: How can Tillich keep this cardinal Christian claim coherently in balance with his doctrine of symbols? For his doctrine of symbols would seem to render his insistence on the necessary facticity of the occurrence of the "New Being" simply another symbol.

As noted, symbols for Tillich arise out of and are expressions of our individual and collective ultimate concerns. Symbols must point beyond themselves in an ecstatic dialectic of high paradox, which logically entails an endless cascade of self-repudiating utterances that can never be objectively grounded and are supremely illustrated in the central "non-symbolic" Tillichian claim "that everything we say about God is symbolic." One might suppose that such a doctrine of symbols would automatically relativize every religious claim and certainly would render purely incidental any particular historical occurrence—such as the concrete appearance of the New Being. Yet, for Tillich, to relativize the Christ event would entail the denial of what he believes to be the central Christian claim.

Often Tillich and Karl Barth are so fundamentally at odds that it is invalid to quote one in conjunction with the other. They operated at different levels of meaning and intent. Usually they

---

24. "Historical Jesus in Paul Tillich's Theology," 144.

stand in naked opposition. However, if only against his own will, Tillich seems to illustrate Barth's contention that only a Docetist, one who believes that Christ was a mere phantom, could deny the necessity of objective God-talk when it comes time to speak of the event of Jesus Christ. As Barth so eloquently proclaims concerning God's ontological reality: "He exists, not only inconceivably as God, but also conceivably as a man; . . . He exists—we cannot avoid this statement; to do so would be the worst kind of Docetism—with objective actuality."[25] It is hard to see how at this point Tillich could seriously deny the point of Barth's Christocentric objectivism especially in the light of Tillich's own credo that it is "the basic Christian assertion that Essential God-Manhood has appeared within existence and subjected itself to the conditions of existence without being conquered by them."[26]

Like his nineteenth-century forebear, Friedrich Schleiermacher, Tillich can be accused of operating out of rationalist and pantheist philosophical presuppositions that preclude his being a Christian. Indeed, Tillich is one of a number of twentieth-century theologians who have actually been read as being thinly disguised atheists. Tillich's whole theology has been interpreted as a tautological smokescreen that hides, perhaps even from himself, the depth of his own religious despair. This is not to subscribe to such a facile reading, but I cannot help but recall Karl Barth's comment about Schleiermacher—whom he always regarded as "a good Christian"—that in order to be a Christian he had to swim against the current of his own thought. This insight can as easily be applied to Tillich.

Nevertheless, Tillich can be a powerful swimmer. When his own Christianity is threatened by the various tides of modern unbelief into which it is frequently carried, or when his system is threatened to be reduced to trivia by its logical drift toward subjectivistic emotivism, Tillich rights himself and finally manages to ground his faith in the concrete reality of the appearance of the

---

25. Barth, *Church Dogmatics*, Vol. IV/2, 50–51.
26. Tillich, *Systematic Theology*, 2:98.

New Being as that New Being lives in Tillich's own Christian self. Thomas J. J. Altizer, in making his glowing tribute to Tillich's influence on his early thinking, finally concluded that he was "forced to resist and oppose Tillich's theological conclusions" as they were "not yet radical enough."[27] Thus, in his own way, Altizer recognized the split in Tillich's theology. Altizer contends "that the real Tillich is the radical Tillich."[28] It is perhaps more prudent to argue that the real Tillich is the Tillich who wrote the books in all their ambiguity, but who at pivotal points concretely grounded his Christian faith in the objective historical reality of "the New Being" despite what such objectivity did for his consistency.

Tillich's Christological retrenchment from his philosophy of religion is also illustrated in his understanding of the cross of Christ. In his discussion of the classic theories of the atonement, he reviews them as insightful symbols, valid not as attempts at an objective explanation of God's purposes in the death of Jesus, but valid in their symbolic functions, that is, as they are reflective of the psychological and existential human needs that are answered by faith in Christ's cross.[29] However, when Tillich expounds his own six "principles of the doctrine of the atonement," we enter again the areas that are at the true center of his own Christological commitments.[30] Interestingly, all reference to "symbols" disappears, and his language takes a decidedly non-symbolic turn.

It is worthwhile to quote Tillich's six principles to see how remarkably objective and seemingly non-symbolic his language becomes. As a reminder, his principles are grounded in what he takes to be the objective, historical *guarantee* provided by our participation in the existential conquest of estrangement by the New Being—Jesus as the Christ.

> The first and all-decisive principle is that the atoning processes are created by God and God alone. . . .

27. Altizer, *Gospel of Christian Atheism*, 10.
28. Ibid.
29. Tillich, *Systematic Theology*, 2:170–76.
30. Ibid., 173ff.

> The second principle for a doctrine of atonement is that there are no conflicts in God between his reconciling love and his retributive justice. . . .
>
> The third principle for a doctrine of the atonement is that the divine removal of guilt and punishment is not an act of overlooking the reality and depth of existential estrangement. . . .
>
> The fourth principle for a doctrine of atonement is that God's atoning activity must be understood as his participation in existential estrangement and its self-destructive consequences. . . .
>
> The fifth principle of a doctrine of atonement is that in the Cross of the Christ the divine participation in existential estrangement becomes manifest. . . .
>
> The sixth principle of a doctrine of atonement is that through participation in the New Being, which is the being of Jesus as the Christ, men also participate in the manifestation of the atoning act of God.[31]

Many philosophers of religion would interpret Tillich's affirmation of the saving significance of the death of Jesus Christ not as the objective truth about an actual act of God, but as simply the historically and culturally conditioned way in which many Western people express their experience of a universally present spiritual dimension of existence that is potentially available to everyone in the world. The divine dimension of Being may be real and universal enough, but as it is sought and experienced by culture-bound human beings it is always expressed in religion in relativizing clouded symbols. Thus, it is not surprising that this universal spirituality might take a Christological form in the faith of Western people just as it takes, for example, a Buddhist or Hindu or Taoist form in the East. Such a view, which has a long pedigree, has been influentially restated by John Hick. From his perspective, the cross of Jesus Christ is finally a symbol for something quite different from that toward which it seems to point. It points not to the God and Father of Jesus Christ but to a reality unknowable except

---

31. Ibid.

in culturally conditioned religious symbols that, though religiously necessary, prove to be as misleading as they are revealing.[32]

For one taking such a line, all religions are relativized in a philosophy of religion which is more comprehensive than any of them, a philosophy of religion that is, to its own satisfaction at least, able to take a more global stance and to understand ultimate reality more clearly and directly than any single religion. For any religion—Christian, Jewish, Hindu, Buddhist, etc.—seen by itself seems to imply a certain exclusivity based upon the religious experience of its adherents.

It is ironic that, finally, in the name of a wider tolerance, the advocates of such a view must implicitly or explicitly say to each and every religion, "We understand your experience in your faith better than you do, for you find the object of your faith standing in some rather direct analogical relationship to the symbols of your faith. Actually, the relationship between your analogies and the truth is at least once removed. Your own theology does not explain your experience as Christian or Buddhist or Hindu. However, *my* philosophy of religion does explain your experience. Thus, all religious analogies, symbols and myths are finally suitable not to the self-understanding of the religionists who created them, but to mine. The ultimate object of *your* faith is not what *you* understand it to be, it is as *I* understand it to be." This in the name of openness and tolerance!

Often, when Tillich wears the robes of a philosopher of religion, it would appear that he cannot escape precisely this sort of relativizing of his own Christianity within the larger context of his general philosophy. Indeed, his definition of religion as "ultimate concern" provides him the conceptual umbrella that allows him summarily to understand all religions better than they understand themselves, i.e., they are not objectively true but are merely symbol systems for expressing the ultimate concern of individuals and communities—God or being-itself, the object of ultimate concern,

---

32. Among his many works see, e.g., Hick's *Interpretation of Religion*, 43-47; and *Metaphor of God Incarnate*.

being literally ineffable. However, not unaware of the seeming contradiction, Tillich also wants to affirm the universal truth of the Christian faith in all its concrete, historical particularity in the very teeth of the scandal created for his philosophy of religion by his insistence that he is above all not a philosopher of religion but a *Christian* apologist.

It is unlikely that anyone will ever be able to sort out the various tensions in Tillich's thought to the general satisfaction of everyone. His whole undertaking is too radically equivocal to allow for such an interpretation. For some, perhaps for many, the very indeterminacy of Tillich's objective intent is his great virtue. To anyone who holds that the mystery of existence lies hidden in an impenetrable fog (or perhaps is the fog itself), Tillich's language might well commend itself. Clearly, Tillich cannot be accused of teaching utterly idiosyncratic novelties, for his doctrine of the self-repudiating narrator of religious symbols bears resemblance to the *via negativa*, the way of negation of the Christian mystical tradition. The way of negation is a route which allows one to speak only of that which God, or the Unconditioned, or the Ground of Being, or the One, is not. For our language arises out of our condition of finitude and therefore can point objectively only to that which is finite.

Certainly the theological reticence of the way of negation serves as a vital reminder to the arrogance of those brands of orthodoxy operating out of a presumptuous cocksureness about the being and doings of God—an attitude which borders on idolatrous blasphemy despite its manifest naïveté. The way of negation can also serve as a reminder against another kind of idolatrous blasphemy born out of a different order of naïveté, that is, the anthropocentrism of liberalism—liberalism which, in Karl Barth's memorable figure, believes it is speaking of "God" when it is merely screaming "Man, Man" at the top of its lungs.

Nevertheless, the corrective implicit in the reluctance of theologies of negation can only be provisional in its usefulness for the proclamation of the Christian faith. If God has become human in the person of Jesus Christ, no human reluctance to engage in speech about God, however well meaning that reluctance may be, can ever justify a final reticence to point directly and objectively to God's genuine appearance in history in the life, death and resurrection of Jesus Christ. As has been shown, Tillich, in his own way, knew this as well as anyone. However, his entire witness to the true appearance of "Essential God-Manhood" has been clouded by his reticence to make his Christological awareness the key to his theological method. Thus, even his witness to the saving work of "Jesus as the Christ" has been obfuscated in a befuddling "pan-symbolism." This has led some to conclude that even his Christological affirmations are really secret denials.

The current theological situation in America bears a deeply Tillichian imprint. Tillich's systematic ambiguity mirrors elements of second-century Gnosticism and ironically creates a bridge between the second-century theological situation and our own. The ancient Gnostics were convinced that the Bible could not be taken on its own terms. The Hellenistic dualism which was so prevalent in the second century, and which the Gnostics took to be a simple given, could not but find the New Testament with its Hebraic roots dangerously materialistic. Doctrines such as the creation, the incarnation, and the death and resurrection of Christ were evidences of the fact that the Old Catholic Church had failed to recognize that which every Gnostic "knew," i.e., that the root of all evil was the material world, that the body was transient and evil while the soul or the spirit alone was eternal and good. Clearly, in the process of combating Gnosticism, the church partook of many elements of the very dualism it fought. Nevertheless, the perseverance of the church in holding that God is the exclusive source of all things in heaven and on earth (creation), that the world is not the handiwork of a fallen and inferior semi-deity, that God sent his Son to live a fleshly human life (he was not a mere phantom), and that the Son of God truly died and was truly risen, are all evidences of the fact that on all the fundamental issues dividing Gnosticism and the church, the church more or less stood its ground.

What was particularly frustrating in the ancient debate from the point of view of those whose faith was tied to the Bible

(Irenaeus being a prime example) was the terminological confusion that ensued during the struggle. The Gnostics used most of the language of the church and biblical tradition; however, that language was used in ways that profoundly altered its original context and meaning. For example, Jesus Christ, the Holy Spirit, the church, the logos, wisdom, life, etc., became what the Gnostics called "eons," transcendent beings who dwelt in the absolutely unreachable heavenly pleroma. Creation became not the act of God, but the morally ambiguous act of an inferior demigod, who himself was an illegitimate offspring of a fallen eon. So it went. Nothing meant what it seemed to mean in its original context.

Such free-flowing reinterpretations—the brilliant juxtaposing of seemingly disparate traditions and elements—syncretism, eclecticism, pluralism—have become the meat and drink of the modern and postmodern world. The *avant-garde* movement, deconstructionism, delights in interpreting the great minds of history against themselves. Nothing is what it seems to be; the question of original intent is sneered at.

Our epoch of Western history has, to be sure, turned Gnosticism on its head and has elevated the body and its sensations above the spirit. In theology, following the larger cultural trend, Sallie McFague, a quintessential academic theologian, deprecates the "model" of God as an invisible spirit and instead remodels God as the body of the world.[33] Such flip-flopping notwithstanding, the basic methodological approach to culture in general and Christianity in particular among many moderns bears an uncanny resemblance to Gnosticism. Were an ancient Gnostic alive today, he or she would be horrified by the modern, hedonistic, materialistic inversion of Gnosticism so common in contemporary anti-traditional theology. But methodologically the Gnostic would have scarce grounds on which to complain. Modern metaphysics has radically changed; indeed, dualism is a dirty word. Still, free interpretation is free interpretation; what's sauce for the goose is sauce for the gander. Postmodernism is simply doing to the bib-

33. McFague, *Models of God*.

lical witness what the matter-hating Gnostic did, only now on a spirit-hating basis.

The comparison to Gnosticism is not self-evidently invidious. Indeed, if one's model of the theological enterprise is that of cultural theology, it is hard to see how one could fault the second-century Gnostics. In the second-century context, the Old Testament's affirmation of the material world was a cultural embarrassment, for this was a dualistic epoch during which there was a strong bias for spirit over matter. Further, the exclusivism of Old Testament faith as it came into the ancient world in its Christianized form might well have seemed out of step in a world that had become increasingly pluralistic and eclectic. Rome, after all, was an empire of many nations. It needed a religion that could provide an ideological unity to support the *Pax Romana*. Perhaps Gnosticism, with its capacity to incorporate and relativize themes and motifs of all religions, was the way to go.

This need was not altogether dissimilar to our current need to support the *Pax Americana*. It is no accident that postmodern theology is so well received in the seminaries and religion departments of the great universities which are our training ground for the young masters of the American Empire. Certainly, seen in the intellectual context of the American university which feeds and tenures it, academic theology which styles itself a "radical" theology is actually a reactionary weather vane blowing with each wind of cultural fashion. Similarly, eclectic Gnosticism might well have seemed to be able to serve the ideals of the Roman Empire and Roman culture better than the doctrinal and exclusive posture of the early Catholic Church. Constantine, of course, did not think so. By the early fourth century, eclecticism had led not to tranquil tolerance but to unresolved spiritual and ultimately political conflict. Constantine bit the bullet and opted in the direction of religious exclusivity. Whether such a policy in the American Empire is even remotely possible is quite another question. Modern Gnosticism of the body can certainly be argued to serve our national and imperialistic ideals of permissive hedonism far better than does historic Christianity. And it can reinterpret all the language and symbols of

Christianity in such a way as to make the tradition itself the lever by which to turn Christianity on its head.

Tillich, far more acutely than his contemporary disciples, felt the tensions between Christ and culture. He wanted both the openness of the unconstrained, speculative, eclectic Gnostic thought and language, on the one hand, and the prophetic iconoclasm and the ultimate truth claims of the Christian tradition on the other. Though Tillich always wanted to both run with the Christian hares and hunt with the worldly hounds, he nevertheless maintained a rather poignant grasp of the difference between hare and hound.

In Tillich's defense, it is simply impossible not to be eclectic. We are all shaped by nature and culture. None of us speaks the language of the angels. Nevertheless, Christianity has always insisted that in the person of Jesus Christ, God has so radically entered into the realm of nature and culture that to those who have eyes to see, there is a third and supremely important given which to some extent permits us to glimpse, however dimly, beyond the limits of our condition as finite, nature and culture-bound creatures. And in the reality of the transcendent who has come upon us, nature and culture are relativized and finally completed.

The most basic question dividing Christian theology today is similar to the issue dividing Christianity in the ancient Gnostic era. Was there a genuine incarnation, a genuine movement of God into our world, or was the Christ a phantom? Or in the case of liberal and postmodern theology, is Christ language merely a Western symbol for a universal, immanent religious and cultural insight? One thing is clear. If there was an actual, objective act of God in the person, work, cross, and resurrection of Jesus Christ, then the intent of Christian language must be an objective one. For God has made himself an object for the world. Yet how can objective discourse be possible given the nature of our finitude and the finite roots of all of our utterances? Before tackling that question, we must first deal with the problem of theological epistemology and the nature of theological speech.

3

Skepticism's Tenuous Reign

THERE WERE many reasons for the reticence of a Bultmann or a Tillich to say in clear and definite words just what it was that they as Christians meant, not just symbolically, but also ontologically when they spoke about God. Bultmann and Tillich have been treated at some length because of their seminal influence on contemporary theology. Examining the theological ambiguity in which such giants seemed to glory puts us in a better position to assess the current movement in the direction of non-objective and non-doctrinal theological discourse.

The cultural influences lying behind the theological mindset of a given era can never totally be separated from those theological concerns generated within the Christian community and that arise out of the faith itself. However, insofar as it is possible to distinguish between cultural influences and the need finally to make more purely theological affirmations, one is tempted to say that, speaking "purely theologically," Bultmann and Tillich, both deeply "cultural" theologians, finally appear more impressed by the awful mystery of God than by the revelational initiative of God as God has acted to overcome the divide between heaven and earth. In fairness to the revelational sensitivity of both men, their final commitment to God's revelation in Jesus Christ led them to assert, however paradoxically, a divine revelatory initiative, but always only after they had seemed to have precluded the very possibility of ontologically objective speech about the divine in-break—this on both philosophic grounds and on the grounds of their respective commitments to the ineffability of God.

To what extent did the reticence of Bultmann and Tillich to affirm unequivocally the ontological reality of divine revelation result from the way in which each of them individually experienced the presence of God in his religious life? To what extent is this reticence the result of the deference they felt toward the claims of modern philosophy and science? It is patently impossible to sort out the answers to such questions. The very fact that it can never be pinpointed precisely where faith experience ends and where the influence of culture begins is a function of a fact that must be beyond dispute; namely, that a Christian is as much a product of his or her culture as is anyone else. Therefore, on the one hand, Christians are those who have in one way or another found themselves, through the person and ministrations of Jesus Christ, brought into their own communal and personal relationships to God. To be sure, they often radically differ as to how they understand the person and ministrations of Jesus Christ. Nevertheless, Jesus Christ is of sufficient significance to them that they are willing to be called by his name. On the other hand, this identification with Jesus Christ does not remove them from the rush of ideas, discoveries, styles, frauds, etc., that bombards them in the culture in rapid-fire succession, nor does identification with Jesus Christ render them immune to the possibility of mistaking their love of culture for their love of him.

There is of course no such thing as a culture-neutral perception. We as twenty-first-century people experience everything—even such universally perceived realities as time and space, cause and effect, and so on—in a manner that has been radically conditioned by our historical, scientific, philosophical, and religious heritage. In the West, for example, with our Einsteinian relativistic worldviews, we can no longer experience time and space in quite the same way as did our immediate cultural forebears, whose perspective was borne of a Newtonian space and time absolutism. If it is the case that our very way of perceiving within our culture is steadily altered by the evolutionary and revolutionary changes in science and philosophy, how much more pronounced are our differences in perceptual perspective from those of people whose cultures developed on different tracks altogether? The data of cultural anthropology, that social science that probes the so-called "primitive" mindset in relation to our own, illustrate abundantly the fact that culture so affects an individual's understanding of what one perceives that it also forms something of the shape and texture of one's perceptions themselves.

Simple common sense, together with the relativizing tendency of contemporary historiography, contemporary philosophical analysis of language, the social sciences, etc., all unite in producing in the ongoing theological enterprise the rather commonplace assumption that we can never fully separate our various individual experiences of the divine from our various individual responses to the constant flux of our culture. Moreover, an analysis of the nature of revelation makes the historical-cultural relativity of revelation even more superabundantly clear, for we know experientially as well as theoretically that our experience of God is never direct.

God, who has made himself known in Jesus Christ, is only known to us through his acts. Thus, we experience God through the realities of this world of which his acts are comprised. Even mysticism, which claims a more "direct" experience, cannot escape such a proviso. When mystics claim intense experiences of God (whatever the source of that experience may ultimately be), what they experience is experienced within the finitude of their consciousness, i.e., they are experiencing their own finite experience, not the interior experience of God. Mysticism *may* be a genuine experience of ultimacy, but all it *can* ever be is a particularly intense experience of what Karl Barth, working from a more orthodox perspective, has called a "secondary objectivity."[1] That is, God is known in his impact upon the finite world, the world of finite nature and the world of finite human experience. In order for us to have a direct experience of ultimacy unmediated by our finite selves experiencing, we would ourselves have to become the consciousness of ultimacy itself. More

1. Barth, *CD*, II/1,16–21.

on this later, but suffice it to say here that this recognition, together with the other limitations just discussed—that our experience of the world about us and our experience of ourselves experiencing are textured and shaped by our cultural preconceptions—are fundamental acknowledgments that we must always keep before us whenever we propose to speak about God.

Thus, while we may revel in the fact that the Christian faith is revelational in its origins, revelation comes to us in a manner and in a context that demands we remain circumspect. Therefore, from every conceivable angle it is abundantly manifest, as Luther insisted, that God as God is in himself must remain hidden to us even in his revelation. God's revelation, always indirect, is a reminder both of his availability to us and his unavailability. The revealed God is also the *deus absconditus,* the abysmally hidden God. Nevertheless, even though we know ourselves to be such seemingly unsuitable receptacles for the divine, not just because of our finitude but because of our sin, we are the "earthen vessels" God has chosen.

Logically, our experience of having any knowledge at all at any level, whether of God, or of a dream, or of a stone, is prior to any philosophical account, any epistemological theory, we may give of such knowledge. Obviously, then, having a theory of knowledge is not a necessary prerequisite for our experiencing what we call knowledge. Epistemologies are devised to account for the knowledge we think we have. Beyond this purely logical priority, it is a given that every theory of knowledge is embedded within the larger context of the total metaphysical and/or theological worldview that undergirds it. Clearly no agreement on the ultimate nature of reality ever has been or ever can be achieved, and thus in the history of philosophy no theory of knowledge can ever hope to sweep the field.

Since all epistemologies are grounded in the world view of given systems, the whole epistemological enterprise must of necessity be splintered. There is no neutral ground on which the epistemological enterprise can stand. And beyond this consideration, every epistemology has its own internal difficulties and vulnerabilities. Ironically, epistemological scrupulosity frequently undercuts the very quest for knowledge that a given philosophic or theological system promises to deliver. Indeed, modern "positivism" from Auguste Comte to logical positivism promised an empirical certainty that it failed to produce, thus calling into question the viability of the metaphysical assumptions on which sub-radical empiricism rests.

Contemporary theology amply demonstrates that excessive concern for epistemology or methodology can stymie all subsequent thought about what is ostensively the very subject matter of theology, i.e., God. Consternation over the impossibility of an airtight account of how we come to know God has in some circles given way to a seemingly genuine despair over the very reality of the knowledge we seemingly thought we had and were thus attempting to give account of. Rather than discarding theories that are abstract and once removed, it is the contemporary mood to discard our very claim to be able to have hold of knowledge—in spite of the fact that the phenomenon of knowing seems to be a concrete and immediate given to our experience. It is ironic that the modern epistemological journey that originally, it was hoped, would lead to the exploration and mapping out of knowledge has led the intellectual establishment into a featureless swamp from which there seems no escape.

Modern epistemology does not tell the whole story of the moralizing, or the noetic, or even the skeptical turn in modern theology; nevertheless, a great deal of modern willingness to embrace an equivocal mode of theological discourse finds many theologians so mesmerized by the vast, seemingly impenetrable modern epistemological morass that they appear intimidated to say what they, in the heart of their faith, believe they know to be true.

This is not the place for a thorough rehearsal of the history of modern epistemology. Nonetheless, a few thumbnail historical observations might be useful in order to convey something of the depth and the diversity of the daunting modern epistemological skepticism that has so contributed to the cultural background against which theology must do its work.

Ever since the eighteenth century and David Hume, the problem of skepticism has troubled the consciences of Western intellectuals. Earlier, Descartes, generally acknowledged as the first "modern" philosopher, had begun by doubting everything so that he could discover that which he could not doubt. He doubted, but in order finally to know. Descartes did not suppose his beginning in skepticism would leave him trapped there.

Hume, on the other hand, began in a positivistic assumption of the self-evident validity of radical empiricism. Finally, however, Hume's positivistic empiricism drove him to a thoroughgoing skepticism. As a radical empiricist, Hume postulated that *all* knowledge comes through the senses, therefore *all* knowledge is *a posteriori*, that is, after the fact of sense perception, and thus all knowledge is reducible to the individual, brute sense perceptions out of which it originally emerged.

While Hume assumed the existence of a material world as the source and object of our sense perceptions, what we can know of that world, he held, is purely perceptual; consequently, we never know what matter or "reality" actually is, or even if our assumption that there actually exists a material world giving rise to our perceptions is true. All that can be known for certain is that there are perceptions. The undeniable givenness of our perceptions did not lead Hume to an empiricist version of the rationalist Descartes' *Cogito, ergo sum*, i.e., *I perceive, therefore I am*. For Hume, not even our egos are empirical perceptions: the self cannot be an empirical object to itself, and therefore even the existence of the ego is thrown into doubt. Both the ontological status of the perceiving self and the world that is being perceived were thus cast into question. Not only was traditional metaphysical (*meta*, meaning "beyond" the physical) knowledge thus rendered impossible, but any claims about the objective status of ethical discourse and certainly theology was viewed by Hume to be empirically incomprehensible. After all, "virtue" or "God" cannot be reduced to empirical perception.

Further, according to Hume, all knowledge being empirical, we obviously do not perceive *necessity* in the interaction of things.

We merely perceive events in constant conjunction. Thus we see a ball rolling on a table and falling off the edge; we perceive the ball rolling, followed by its falling, but we do not *perceive* a necessary connection between the two occurrences. Indeed we could even imagine in our mind's eye the ball not falling but merely floating in air. Therefore, the ball's not falling entails no contradiction. For Hume, the only thing that can be styled a contradiction is that which cannot be imagined, e.g., a round square. Thus, the falling of the ball cannot be said to be empirically or rationally necessary. All we can finally say logically is that in the past we have empirically observed that objects free in space always have fallen, and thus as a matter of what is finally pure habit of mind we assume they will always fall in the future. The so-called necessity behind even so seemingly rational constructs as the laws of nature is really our logically crude assumption that future cases will resemble past ones. In short, this is the "logic" of bias.

Such argumentation serves to undercut any notion of the necessity of cause and effect. Thus, since we can have no empirical certainty as to what is the "really real," and not even a logical ground for arguing the necessity of cause and effect—as so-called necessity proves to be a mere habit of mind—rational confidence in the certitude of all of our knowledge, be it scientific, metaphysical, theological, ethical or even psychological, is fundamentally shaken.

Ironically, Hume had a high regard for science and a deep respect for Sir Isaac Newton. Nevertheless, the argumentation Hume mustered against all "superstitions" (natural theology) and all other "delusions," such as the belief one can do "metaphysics," appeared also to undercut the rational certitude of his revered science itself.

So thoroughly did Hume do his work that even the great attempt of Immanuel Kant to answer Hume granted so much to Hume's skepticism that in the end for Kant the necessities of knowledge, such as cause and effect, were not grounded in the *noumenal* world, i.e., in things themselves, but in the *phenomenal* world, i.e., the world of our minds. Kant argued that while *a posteriori* we empirically perceive the raw data from the noumenal world, these data only come to consciousness after they have been structured through *a priori* categories of the mind. Thus our knowledge *must* be orderly and necessarily regular, because our consciousness receives the data of our senses pre-structured—inalterably categorical. Since the categories of the mind include cause and effect, we can be certain of the necessity of cause and effect. This is not because cause and effect are metaphysical properties of the world "out there" but because our minds order the raw data of that world for our understanding of it. The noumenal world for Kant, following Hume, is metaphysically unknowable.

Indeed, it was on the basis of the fact that the "real" world may be quite different than it appears to us in our categorical perceptions of it that Kant thought it impossible to assert the existence of other minds, human freedom, immortality and God. We can never, on the basis of theoretical certainty, hold to such things. Indeed, the idea of freedom, for example, contradicts our empirical experience, for if the world were, in fact, as bound by the rigid structures of cause and effect by which the world is represented to us in our understandings, there could be no freedom. However, that we do not perceive the world in terms of freedom—but rather in terms of the unyielding categories of cause and effect—does not prove that the world as it actually is in itself corresponds to our noetically structured perception of it. The world in its actual ontological reality may indeed be governed by its own spontaneity and not by cause and effect at all.

Therefore, since it is of considerable working importance that we believe in freedom, together with such things as other minds, a world beyond our perception, immortality and God, and since the world as it is in itself, in spite of our perceptions, may, noumenally, afford the possibility of such things, we can postulate them as matters of "practical reason," held not as rational propositions, but as articles of faith.

In attempting to save science from skepticism, and religion and ethics from both science and skepticism, but grounding much of his affirmations in the unknowability of the metaphysical truth of things, Kant opened the door to extreme skepticism such as that of his radical disciple, Hans Vaihinger, who insisted that *all* of our so-called knowledge was merely a series of "useful fictions" that we hold "as if" they were true. Kant would not have approved of this conclusion, but it's hard to see how he could have resisted it.

One way around this skeptical impasse was the way of idealism. Hume's empiricist predecessor, George Berkeley, foreseeing the abject skepticism that empiricism would lead to if it persisted in the assumption that there exists an unknowable material "world out there," went the way of idealism. For Berkeley, since our minds only perceive ideas, all we can properly claim to know anything about are ideas. The postulation of matter is a useless philosophical abstraction that has no basis in experience. Since we can only affirm the existence of that which we perceive, only ideas exist. The world is real enough. Indeed, God perceives the world into being. Thus, the world is supremely permanent and stable, for it is comprised of God's ideas. When we perceive empirical reality, we are in fact perceiving directly that which alone exists, that is, God's own thoughts. Hume responded to such idealism by acknowledging it will be unanswerable, but it is also, for most people, on the face of it, unbelievable.

The same can be said for those nineteenth-century versions of idealism supremely illustrated by Friedrich Hegel. Hegel resorted to the extremity of absolute idealism to counter the skepticism implicit in Kant. But he produced a system that, for many, was finally more unbelievable than the skepticism it was designed to counter.

Modern existentialism, either in its Christian form (Søren Kierkegaard) or in its nihilistic form (Friedrich Nietzsche), rather than agonize over this metaphysical impasse, granted, in fact demanded, the sheer impossibility of metaphysical knowledge if there is to be any honest human knowledge. Our metaphysical incapacity was, in Kierkegaard's case, seen as a function of the fact that we are finite; moreover, our metaphysical systems, which imply a finality that only God could possibly have, are presumptuous. Of course, for Kierkegaard there is a "system," but it is known only to God. In the case of Nietzsche, it was impossible because God is dead, and thus there exists no truth, no values, and no reality except as the *Übermensch* who, by an arbitrary act of will asserts his own truths, values, and realities.

On the other extreme, also holding that there can be no post-Humeian metaphysics, philosophers of a more scientific bent have asserted various forms of scientistic positivism. The position known as logical positivism went so far as to claim that only those statements that can be empirically verified, or those statements that are true by definition, i.e., tautologies, make any real sense at all. Theology, ethics, metaphysics, aesthetics, etc., were relegated either to the limbo of "emotivism" or the hell of "meaninglessness." Logical positivism has been largely discredited, if only because the system cannot meet its own criteria of meaning—for how can one empirically demonstrate that statements are meaningful if and only if they can be empirically verified or are tautologies? Nevertheless, there remain many closet logical positivists among those philosophers who are generally described as being members of the British and American school of "linguistic analysis."

Language analysts and those philosophers whose roots are in existentialism rarely relate to one another philosophically. Indeed, the two schools stand in long-term antipathy to one another. The atheism, ethical nihilism, and metaphysical skepticism that so often characterize *both* schools are grounded in such radically different assumptions as to appear to cancel each other out. Jean-Paul Sartre, for example, regarded atheism as the pivotal, moral turning point of his whole philosophy. Logical positivists, on the other hand, regard the whole moral dispute between atheism and theism to be a nonsensical confusion. Nevertheless, the fact that modern schools cannot agree on the grounds for theological and metaphysical despair tends, in the long run, simply to underscore the radical, skeptical malaise that characterizes much Western intellectualism, be it atheistic or theistic. Certainly, such a confusion in the camp of the enemy is nothing in which Christian theology can take comfort since clearly both camps despise Christianity even more than they despise each another.

Karl Marx and Sigmund Freud might at first glance provide some kind of buffer against the tides of modern skepticism.

Though they shared very few common assumptions with reference to the fundamental human predicament, both Marx and Freud had no lack of confidence as to their epistemological grasp of the realities of things. Both believed that they were taking "scientific" hold of their subjects—the historical, economic order in Marx's case, the human psyche in Freud's. However, both regarded "scientific" atheism as a prerequisite to the overcoming of human woes, insofar as they believed those woes could be overcome. For Marx, religion was an opiate that was used by the ruling class to still the revolutionary outrage of the underclass. For Freud, religion was an infantile delusion, a neurotic refusal to face the bleak realities of human mortality. In any case, atheism was fundamental to both. The methodology of both Marx and Freud prescribed their reading of not just religion but metaphysics, ethics, and art as well, for all such human undertakings were to be looked at not for what they appear to be saying, but to expose a cover-up. Religion, metaphysics, ethics, and art all function as masks for the ideological class interests or the subconscious psychological states of those who invent them. Clearly, therefore, the task of the enlightened interpreter, employing what is presently dubbed the "hermeneutics of suspicion," is skeptically to expose the deception behind every *prima facie* ethical, metaphysical and theological claim. Such a hermeneutical undertaking further entails a revisionist reassessment of the whole Western "canon" of art and literature in order to lay bare the bias lurking in and behind it.

Marxism and Freudianism are of course elaborate belief systems, but they lay hold to so intolerant and exclusivistic a claim to the truth of things that they must of necessity attack to the death all alternative claims, thus creating in the true adherent an attitude of skepticism, if not cynicism, toward every other way of thinking. If one can buy into either belief system, one's skeptical problems are over, for one *has* the only objective hold on truth. However, twenty-first-century thinking has produced fewer and fewer mainline Marxist or Freudian orthodoxies but rather a highly selective, eclectic use of these monolithic, fundamentally mutually exclusive systems, the result among many intellectuals being a general cynicism concerning almost everything—here on Marxian, there on Freudian grounds—without the compensation of a coherent belief system to put such skepticism in perspective.

In other cases, the eclectic use of the cynical legacy of Marx and Freud has been harnessed to new ideologies by which the whole of Western civilization can be exposed for its repressive biases. In the case of feminism, for example, the bias is patriarchy. Without denying that there is a large grain of truth in feminism, or for that matter in Marxism or Freudianism, the proliferation of such ideologies, each prefaced by such all-encompassing, all destructive hermeneutics, has simply served to fill the air with mutually exclusive "truths" that cannot finally establish themselves except on the graves of all other "truths." Ironically, the very proliferation of absolute truth systems prepares the ground for the triumph of an absolute skepticism.

A recent skeptical fashion is "deconstructionism" (fathered by Jacques Derrida, Paul De Man, et al.). Deconstructionism stands above all in the spirit of Nietzsche in his denial that there exists any objective truth or reality. Nietzsche claimed that philosophy has been one long conspiracy to hide this nihilistic "truth" by using what finally amounts to mere metaphorical images as if they had some objective significance. Deconstructionism claims that not just written documents but all things human, all history, even our grasp of nature, are "texts" to be interpreted in such a way as to expose the various "metaphors" and "tropes" of which these "texts" are comprised. Once the metaphorical character of all language—perhaps particularly philosophical language—is exposed for the mass of figurative metaphors it is, the groundlessness of metaphysical or theological claims is exposed.

However, given the very character of language, deconstructionists acknowledge that every statement implies "meaning," thus a metaphysical frame of reference to some extent cannot be avoided. It is one of the paradoxes that deconstructionism is prepared to live with. Nevertheless, if the metaphysical implication cannot be fully avoided, one need not capitulate to it. Every statement must forever be deconstructed and deconstructed again and again so as to constantly expose the false suggestion that our "texts" grow out of an actual encounter with some alleged "reality" to which they give objective witness, a so-called presence or truth. This process is never ending.

In sketching out this wide range of modern skeptical options, it must not be overlooked that each approach has preserved for itself, as it must, vital areas of "belief"—even if it is belief in the final "truth" of skepticism—that somehow is retained against the general modern deluge of uncertainty and pluralism. Inevitably some necessary bit of ground on which to stand is preserved, without which it would be impossible to achieve the leverage necessary to topple the "deluded" beliefs of others. Though the very contradictions within modern skepticism tend to cancel out any coherent skeptical consensus, this confusion should give theology no cause for rejoicing. The very fact of pluralistic chaos feeds the underlying skeptical ethos of our age and appears to foster the paradoxical "certitude" that, in truth, metaphysical, moral, aesthetic and theological truth cannot be known.

Hume, writing with some relish, seemed to see this situation coming. He was speaking specifically of the skeptical implications arising out of the fact that various natural theologies were in radical conflict, but what he said of natural theology can just as easily be argued against any and all systems or even anti-systems of thought, philosophical or theological, as they conflict with one another:

> All religious systems, it is confessed, are subject to great and insuperable difficulties. Each disputant triumphs in his turn; while he carries on an offensive war, and exposes the absurdities, barbarities, and pernicious tenets of his antagonist. But all of them, on the whole, prepare a complete triumph for the Sceptic, who tells them, that no system ought ever to be embraced with regard to such subjects: For this plain reason, that no absurdity ought ever to be assented to with regard to any subject. A total suspense of judgement is here our only reasonable resource. And if every attack, as is commonly observed, and no defence, among theologians, is successful, how complete must be *his* victory, who remains always, with all mankind, on

the offensive and has himself, no fixed station or abiding city, which he is ever, on any occasion, obliged to defend?[2]

Christian theology runs the risk of losing its own soul when, in response to the skeptical chiding of a David Hume, it self-defensively attempts to strike back by exploiting the merely logical inconsistencies and incoherence of skepticism. To be sure, it is patently obvious that the skeptical credo, "I *know* that I cannot *know*," is problematic. For if I *know* that I cannot know, then, in fact, I know everything that can and needs be known. And how can anyone be believed in his or her claim to know so very much without being obliged to prove the case by using the very reason that skepticism has called into doubt? It is certain no skeptic ever claimed that he or she did not have knowledge while leaving open the possibility that others might have knowledge. Skepticism is as imperialistic as any other ideology or system. It carries with it, in all its negations, the positive certainty that the universe is such that all subjects metaphysical, religious or ethical are impenetrable conundrums, that any attempts to penetrate them are delusions, and that this is the case not just for the skeptic, but for everyone else as well.

Skepticism's ultimate incoherence is so apparent that it cannot help but be noticed and discussed, but theology must do so only in the humbling realization that any attempt to argue skepticism to its knees must inevitably fail on every front. Above all there seems an inherent contradiction in pointing to the universal saving significance of Christ's self-sacrificing cross with one hand and then with the other hand engaging in an aggressive or defensive apologetic war against the unbelief of the humanity for whom Christ died. Not only is such a war fought with the world's own weapons in the name of the self-giving Christ somewhat paradoxical, but it is war that presently offers not even an illusion of victory. For in the present climate, skepticism gathers strength from the fact that every counterargument seems to underscore the disarray of the modern epistemological situation. The very nature of modern doubt is such that it feeds even upon the logic of its own refutation.

2. Hume, "Dialogues Concerning Natural Religion," 88–89.

The most that we can or should hope might result from a modest pointing-up of the difficulties so clearly inherent in modern skepticism is that perhaps such a recognition will help to encourage Christian theologians not to lose heart. Theology need not abjectly rush to surrender (as sadly it often seems all too willing to do) to the worldliness of a world that is itself lost in confusion.

But even this consideration must be tempered by an even more critical recognition. The greatest "enemy" of the Christian faith is not the self-professed unbeliever, but that far more subversive unbeliever who lives within the breast of every believing Christian. It would be madness to assume that any Christian is immune to the doubts of the age, to say nothing of doubt that arises out of one's personal story. It is precisely the Christian living out his or her personal and cultural unbelief, far more than the non-Christian or the post-Christian skeptic, who has the greatest potential for subverting the word of Christ.

We all know the phenomenology of our personal doubt all too well. How quickly my own faith dwindles into doubt only to be rekindled, only to lead again into renewed doubt. So often God's hiddenness and silence are so daunting that I dread that perhaps it is in fact the truth, as the skeptics claim, that my faith in God is delusion. And does not the very impenetrability of so-called ultimate questions make the accomplishments of what *can* be known all the more impressive? As my secular friends remind me, in science and technology we see what the human mind *can* penetrate and master. Given the incredible accomplishments of technology, what sense is there in seeking meaning in a primal unknown? Surely I would never want to live in a primitive, pre-scientific society in which existence is constantly plunged into the primal unknown. I value the life and security provided for me by technology and science. I work many hours a week so as to acquire the technical means to live "well" in the contemporary sense of the word. Science and technology, to judge by how I serve them and am served by them, are my gods. Does the god of my secularity even permit belief in a living God? I must own my god. Yet it is so often an empty god, and I find that when I remember the God who is the God of my heart of hearts I really do not believe in the god of this world. In my heart of hearts I truly believe in the God of Jesus Christ. And 'round and 'round it goes. As Kierkegaard described the torrent of his own doubt, the image is conjured of the overdrive that precedes meltdown.

> My doubt is terrible—Nothing can withstand it—it is a cursed hunger and I can swallow up every argument, every consolation and sedative—I rush at 10,000 miles a second through every obstacle.[3]

Were the bulwark of the Christian faith either the present pluralistic state of Western cultural uncertainty or the believer's mercurial stream of consciousness, Christianity would die the death of a thousand self-contradicting objections and affirmations.

Beset by personal ambivalence and sometimes despite myself, feeling intimidated by the anti-Christian hostility of modern culture, I must confess a certain primal sympathy for the revelational positivism of one like Kierkegaard, who, seeing the morass into which the modern epistemological quest must lead, observed that the only way to deal with post-Kantian skepticism is to "break with it."[4] By this Kierkegaard meant that finally the Christian faith is exclusively revelatory.[5]

---

3. Kierkegaard, *Kierkegaard Anthology*, 14. Kierkegaard's sense of desperation is born of the fact that the doubter is also always the believer and vice versa. We are rarely at peace with either our doubt or our faith.

4. Kierkegaard, *Concluding Unscientific Postscript*, 292: "A skepticism which attacks thought itself cannot be vanquished by thinking it through, since the very instrument by which this would have to be done is in revolt. There is only one thing to do with such a skepticism, and that is to break with it."

5. Kierkegaard, *On Authority and Revelation*. As translator Walter Lowrie observes in his preface, this work decisively corrects the "common complaint that S. K.'s greatest defect was his 'subjectivity,' his blindness to anything objectively given in Christianity" (xliv). However, it must be acknowledged that there were, in effect, two Kierkegaards concerning the question of the objective givenness of Christianity. There is the existentialist, radically subjectivistic Kierkegaard, who spoke of Christian faith as the product of a crisis of personal existence which drove the individual to a dramatic "leap" out into the darkness, and Kierkegaard the fideist. The existentialist side is, of course, the side of Kierkegaard that Bultmann and Christian existentialism

Indeed Kierkegaard when pressed could be so radically revelational in his understanding of the foundations of Christian authority that he would not only remove completely the central claims of the Christian faith from the realm of philosophical-epistemological argumentation and debate, but also, it would seem, from the realm of in depth subjective self-examination, which was the hallmark of his existentialism—as, for example, on the question of eternal life:

> A Christian priest, if he would speak correctly, must say quite simply, "We have Christ's word for it that there is an eternal life—therewith the matter is decided. Here there is no question either of racking one's brains or about speculation, but about the fact that it is Christ who said it, not in the capacity of a profound thinker, but with his divine authority." Let us go further, let us assume that there is an eternal life because Christ has said it, so believingly he circumvents all the profundity and pondering and fathoming wherewith people rack their brains. On the other hand, let us take one who wants to rack his brains profoundly with the question about immortality—I wonder if he will have a right to deny that the simple assertion is a profound answer to the question? What Plato says about immortality is really profound, won by deep pondering—but poor Plato had no authority whatsoever.[6]

Kierkegaard was not wrong in his core insistence that in the first place and in the last place the authority of Christianity to make claims about the truth of God stands or falls on its contention that God has revealed himself decisively in the person of Jesus Christ. If God was indeed in Jesus Christ, then the reality toward which Christianity points, in all the diversity of its theological witness, is genuine. If God was not in Jesus Christ, then Christianity is,

---

took up and that is so ripe for the Feuerbachian reduction process, i.e., faith seen as a human attempt to cope with existential desperation is thereby reduced to its essence in human experience. The fideist side of Kierkegaard is represented by his radical stress on revelation and the objectivity of the divine initiative in Christ. While Kierkegaard never systematically worked out the tension between his existentialism and his revelational fideism, any attempt to stress the former to the exclusion of the latter is decidedly un-Kierkegaardian.

6. Ibid., 115–16.

of course, reinterpretable into a culturally congenial philosophy (i.e., any philosophy imaginable and its opposite). However, it is hardly worth preserving given how little in Christianity's doctrinal reservoir is ever actually congenial to the spirit of our age or of any other age, and how much must be jettisoned or drastically reinterpreted in order to save the few supposedly congenial fragments.

Christianity's only excuse is that in spite of the various ways Christians have sought in each age to find in it congenial elements for that age (thus distorting it according to the style of each successive age), it is, nonetheless, utterly no thanks to Christians that God was in Jesus Christ. It would be intolerable for people of decency to be anything but Christianity's implacable foes, were it guilty, as it has been, of such monstrosities as heresy trials, inquisitions, complicity in slavery, exploitation of the poor, pogroms, the liberal rationale for the West's colonial exploitation of the developing nations, etc., and then, to cap it all off, finally, niceties aside, it were a lie.

Quite apart from any epistemological considerations, rather on the basis of its moral right to exist, the Christian faith must point, however deeply humiliated over the wretchedness of its betrayals it may be, to Jesus Christ as its sole authority, and complete reason for being.

Standing on such a ground it is possible even to feel quite heady and to argue that the whole question of philosophical epistemology is thus, finally, quite beside the point. Christ is the self-proved foundation of our faith. Indeed, the only way to deal with human skepticism *is* as Kierkegaard declared, to break with it and live in the irresolvable tension that though children of culture, Christian faith requires that we must resolutely try to stand against the tide of culture. This line has a certain almost inescapable logical force, and there have been historical moments (e.g., the anti-apologetic posture of the 1934 Barman confession that pitted the Confessing Church against the culturally dominant Nazi philosophy and myth) when this exclusivistic path seemed the only faithful way to go.

Nonetheless, such a radical fideist posture pursued with unflinching radicality in each and every context finally pushes the

Christian into an unbearable schizophrenia. Even one's most personal existential experiences of both faith and doubt are culturally conditioned. Even Kierkegaard in his recounting the sorts of doubts that raced through his mind showed that he knew this. An unwavering fideism cannot but fail to take to heart that we are all, each of us, incarnated not in a vacuum but in culture. Thus, we are caught in the apologetic dialogue whether we wish to be or not. Notwithstanding Tertullian's opposition to philosophy, Tertullian himself, as has frequently been observed, was deeply indebted to philosophy, particularly Stoicism, as when, for example, he resorted to the materialistic language of the Stoics in his description of the three persons of Trinity as being one in "*substance*."[7] To say nothing of his Hellenistic philosophic prejudices that led him to passionately deny that God could suffer. Nor is it to be forgotten that such modern anti-apologists as Kierkegaard and Barth were highly sophisticated, "cultured" modern men.

---

7. This is forcefully illustrated by Tertullian even against his will. His position as the first radical fideist among systematic theologians is well-established. "What is there in common between Athens and Jerusalem? What between the Academy and the Church? What between heretics and Christians? . . . Away with all projects for a 'Stoic,' a 'Platonic' or a 'dialectic' Christianity! After Christ Jesus we desire no subtle theories, no acute enquiries after the gospel. . . ." From chapter seven of "On Prescription Against Heretics," in Bettenson, *Documents of the Christian Church*, 6.

4

Theology and the Language It Must Speak

A Christianity that is obedient to the biblical witness must, of necessity, recognize that it is a theological religion: "And the Word became flesh and lived among us, full of grace and truth; we have beheld his glory, glory as of the only Son from the Father."[1] Christianity, if it is to be faithful to the glory *it* has beheld, must always be willing to witness boldly and with unequivocal clarity concerning its objective intent. For while it is true enough that "now we see in a mirror dimly,"[2] the fact remains that "it is God the only Son, who is close to the Father's heart, who has made him known."[3] If it is the case that the very *Logos*, who is the word, wisdom, reason, and thought of God, has been made manifest in the person of Jesus Christ, then Christianity has a great deal to talk about—far more than it can ever think to say. By the very example of his *kenosis*, Jesus Christ demonstrated that he did not come into the world with the intention of blinding us in the brilliance of his superior wisdom, leaving us stupefied and silent. By his self-humbling he granted us access to the heart of God. He gave up even the certain knowledge of his own being as God's Son, that the knowledge of his servant divinity might be ours.

We have seen how such eminent theological figures as Rudolf Bultmann and Paul Tillich were in many ways Christian theolo-

---

1. John 1:14. Revised Standard Version.
2. 1 Cor 13:12.
3. John 1:18.

gians at war with their own philosophies. Their Christological commitments compelled them to affirm God's genuine self-giving in spite of the fact that their naturalistic and existentialist philosophical biases required of them a distressing agnosticism concerning the possibility of straightforward testimony to that self-giving.

Many contemporary inheritors of the mantle of Bultmann and Tillich do not share their deep Christological faith; and thus, lacking a Christological foundation, they find themselves wholly without a basis on which to speak with theological independence to their philosophical-cultural situation. Indeed, if God was not uniquely manifested in Jesus Christ, then it is difficult to see how Christian theology could have anything to say that would not seem superfluous in the contemporary climate.

Neo-liberal theology, generally speaking, has imagined that the problem of speaking a unique and relevant word to the pluralistic, postmodern world is above all an epistemological one—thus the current obsessive preoccupation with method among theologians, and the seemingly endless tinkering with a discipline (epistemology) that, in spite of the allure of its fascination and its pretense to exactitude, is finally the most unsatisfying and paradoxical of sciences. Insofar as epistemology reigns as the queen of even the secular humanities, all subjects are thereby reduced to it, and the whole humanistic intellectual enterprise is threatened by triviality, self-absorption, and nihilism. However, when Christian theology plays this epistemological game, how else can the clear-headed atheist see it except as a hidden, even self-deceived acknowledgment of an atheism at theology's heart? Modern atheism is not impressed with and will not be converted by the constant fine-tuning of theologians who feel they dare not speak a substantive word unless with phobic scrupulosity they take account of every jot and tittle in the ever-changing repertoire of modern skepticism. How can anyone resist the surmise that that which cannot be discussed except in extreme circumspection does not actually exist? Hear these taunts from the quarters of atheism:

> Theology since Barth has been consumed with the "therapeutic" task of clarifying its own logic and surveying its domains

of discourse. Such narcissism of method, nonetheless, is but a backhanded recognition of the point Derrida emphasizes. If theology, instead of examining the nature and attributes of God, or even exploring the meaning and discursive function of the holy name, becomes preoccupied in contrast with pondering the purpose for which it is "done," then it must come to understand itself *strictu sensu* as a meditation within discourse upon discourse. The divine word, the *sacra verba*, is truly made flesh; it reaches its kenotic consummation, its radical otherness, in a theology which is naught but a writing about theology.[4]

How almost inexpressibly ironic it is that nihilistic champions of the death of God, the demise of man, and the ultimate emptiness of being like Carl Raschke or Mark C. Taylor should express themselves not just with rhetorical flourish and dash but also in a fundamentally straightforward, clearly rational, and determinate manner! A reading of Taylor's work may leave one with questions as to his ultimate motives, the adequacy of his claims, and the internal legitimacy of his writing at all, but there can be little question as to the basic import of what he is claiming to be objectively true: Taylor simply doesn't believe in the existence of God, and he doesn't believe the enlightened *cognoscenti* of postmodern culture believe in God either.[5] And since Western civilization has grounded its beliefs about reality and humanity in the God hypothesis, the whole of Western culture as well as the self-understanding of individuals in that culture must be stripped bare and forced to see both the hypocrisy and the incurably fluid state of affairs that result for all subsequent thought and discourse. All this is clear—fair enough. There is enough of a straightforward hypothesis here that it is possible to agree or disagree. Personally, I do both. No one could, I think, attend to Taylor's or Raschke's texts and conclude that the very timidity of their atheistic claims reveal that in fact they were hidden fundamentalists.

However, apart from the irony of the fact that such champions of indeterminacy write in so determinate a manner—alas, there

---

4. Carl A. Raschke, "Deconstruction of God," 14.
5. Taylor, *Erring*.

seems to be no other way to be understood!—the supreme *theological* irony is that those who believe in nothing do not equivocate in their atheism, postpone interminably their discourse about (not) God, or substitute method for content. Rather, they say what they mean. On the other hand, damningly, many theologians who claim to still believe in the reality of reality and the validity of God-talk tergiversate, hedge, qualify, and apostrophize, presumably in the desperate hope that by remaining ever so still in the water their faith either will go unnoticed or will seem so unexceptional that it might save them from being devoured by the skeptical sharks of every size and species swimming all about them.

This is not to suggest that a changeless orthodoxy is the answer to modern pluralism and nihilism. Not even in orthodox eras was orthodoxy changeless. For while Jesus Christ is, indeed, the same yesterday and today and forever, we change (while remaining in many ways the same), and therefore our witness to him and our rational, doctrinal thought about him must be vigorously re-argued and recast in each generation. Theology, as Barth once noted, is not done for posterity. Granted, in each generation there are "hot" issues and therefore not every generation can or will totally re-examine every aspect of the faith with equal rigor. However, the work of rejuvenation must go on. Theological activity is a sign of life in the church. Such intellectual vigor is not the only sign, to be sure. Ethical integrity and evangelism are other such signs. But it *is* one such vital sign. When the church tries to repeat the formulas of the past without the scrutiny and constructive restatement that grow from a vital encounter with the present, something is amiss. Christian theology must, as of first importance, keep open the channels between the root convictions of the Christian faith and the working assumptions, the presuppositions, the needs, the fears, the hopes, and the doubts of living people. Herein lie both the privilege and the peril that confront the theological enterprise. On the one hand, it is the privilege of theology to offer itself as the servant of both Christian and non-Christian humanity as that humanity seeks to plumb the most fundamental questions of faith and existence. Theology offers this small service to humanity because it first of all serves that greater servant who is the very Word of God.

However, as it serves that Word, theology has potentially more to say than any ear can hear. Therefore, knowing it cannot even begin to say all that God's word inspires, its witness must be ordered by an agenda relevant to its situation. In a fundamental sense, theology does not set its own agenda. The agenda of theology is set for it in the constantly changing interface between the word of God as that word is the servant Lord of the world and the world itself in its discrete cultural-historical situations. Were the world not constantly posing new questions in the context of inexorable historical change, there would be no need for theology, for then history would not have evolved, and we could simply repeat the words that were sufficient for the first century. Theology arises when people, both inside and outside the church, in either a friendly or a hostile manner, inquire from the point of view of their inescapable contemporaneity as to what the Bible and the ancient creeds are all about and whether and in what way they are believable.

Not so very long ago it was fashionable to speak of the need for theology to be "relevant" to the world. Much of such talk was highly self-congratulatory. Behind it lay the assumption that *I* am the relevant one and those who speak about other matters—who have other concerns—are "irrelevant." Frequently the fact was overlooked that most of our utterances are probably irrelevant or relevant in ways we cannot know. The agenda of Jesus Christ in the world is often hard to locate and even harder to honor. To actually have been genuinely relevant to that agenda is not, as a matter of the first order, the result of our insight or good intentions. It is, purely and simply, a miracle of grace. As one strives to be in phase with the agenda of Jesus Christ in the world, one does so with clay feet, and the pitfalls others have fallen into are always, ironically, far clearer for us to see than those into which we ourselves are tumbling. There is much pride in theology but also great insecurity. I suspect that most theologians fly back and forth in their consciousness from self-congratulatory certitude to abject self-pity and despair, wondering if they say anything worth hearing, if their message is not finally either an anachronism, a superfluity, or a betrayal. Theologians labor at writing books and articles that they convince themselves are quite relevant—only to find them politely received and casually forgotten.

Theology moves between the Scylla of anachronistic repristination and the Charybdis of craven accommodation. No doubt everyone has experienced moments in which an ancient text suddenly becomes alive and relevant as no contemporary text can. One hopes that every Christian has such moments with the Bible. Certainly a new vision of the faith that has no sympathy for—that makes no creative use of—the ancient wisdom of the church is, on the face of it, a heresy. But even if the great mass of people are fully capable of moments of great sympathy for the richness of the past—take for example the great public interest in art museums—it is difficult for people to find the key to their present lives in a past that for all its richness is dead. Nevertheless, one of the temptations of theologians in having been edified by the classic moments of the Christian past, in having pored over the works of the giants, is to be deceived into the romantic hope that there can be a repristination, that the answer to the crying need of the present is some kind of revival of Luther, Calvin, Wesley, Thomas, the fathers, the primitive church, et al. Such repristination may produce academic fads or sectarian moments satisfying to an elite few. But it is inevitably a dead end.

Another saying of George Santayana has become something of a cliché: that those who do not learn from history are doomed to repeat it. Though there rings in it a note of truth, it supposes that the lessons of history are clearly evident to those who seek their wisdom. In fact, the past as it exists in the shadow world of the reconstructions we call "history" is very difficult to bring into our contemporary context and grasp sufficiently that it might instruct us. Whether we like it or not, we are being driven into the future, the only place where God's ultimate truth and purpose will ever be in view. To be sure, these are not modern acknowledgments. They are all already present in Augustine, the first historical Western thinker.

Clearly the theological right's repristination of ancient orthodoxy is an illusion. However, this does not justify the accommodating impulse of the theological left, which would uncritically baptize each new wave of human culture just as nineteenth-century liberalism characteristically did. It is in the very willingness of theology to find its agenda in the interface between Jesus Christ and the world that it *ought* to recognize, but so rarely does, that Christianity must not only resist baptizing but must even vigorously oppose many fundamental stances of the prevailing culture.

All such judgments are rarely obvious, except perhaps in hindsight. Where does faithful commitment to God's revelation in the history of Israel, old and new, ossify into an anachronistic orthodoxy, or worse, into a formal confessionalism that hides its doubt behind the words of ancient creeds only a fraction of which it believes? Where does uncritical, unprophetic openness to the present movement of God degenerate into a *de facto* denial of Jesus Christ?

Beyond this, it is a statistical certainly that most, if not all, theological statements are in error. This is the obvious logical corollary of the fact that there is such radical disagreement among theologians. Not only is the very object of theology frequently in dispute—indeed, wildly divergent perspectives press their cases, perspectives ranging from the extremes of theological atheism to hyper-fundamentalism—but even within a given school or a denomination there is often radical and vociferous disagreement on the specifics of doctrine and ethics. It follows that even if there is the possibility of being "right," only a very few could be "right" by the logical principle of the mutual exclusion of opposites.

All this I take as a counsel not of despair, but of liberation. What a relief that we are not required to be right! For if we were, no one would be saved. Theologians, like all of us, are sinners saved by grace. Indeed, though they prove themselves obtuse blunderers when confronted by the mystery of God, God suffers these fools—and even redeems their insights—gladly. Luther's advice to sin boldly—God can forgive a bold sinner—fully applies to theology. Theologize boldly! God can forgive bold theology. Just as he can use us in the boldness of our sin to a redemptive purpose, so his word can shine through the haze of our insights.

We are liberated from the unbearable obligation of doctrine conceived as the unvarnished truth about God. Doctrine is rather the attempt of the church to say as directly and objectively as possible what it means when it witnesses to God. God has revealed himself, and thus the church not only has something it might say, but something it *must* say. It is downright odd that we have convinced ourselves that we are philosophically or culturally constrained from saying it. God risked all in the *kenosis* of his Son. Can we not hazard ourselves to God's glory? As Karl Barth so passionately witnessed to the freedom and joy of theological witness:

> As God wills man to be free before Him, He always has in view the freedom of those who have something to relate about Him, the freedom of confessors who cannot keep silence but must speak of Him, their freedom to expose themselves to His glory, to commit themselves to His honour with clear and definite words, to be serviceable to Him in and with these words, to be His declared and decided partisans.[6]

This is not to deny that like any other discipline, theology inevitably must develop its own technical language with all its subtleties, allusions, "in" jokes, and even neologisms; nor is it to decry that such language will be comprehensible only to those who have labored long in the trade. The very nature of specialization is such that it needs the exactitude and nuance that jargon can provide. However, specialization too often leads to a ranging far afield from the actual subject that the specialist seeks to understand. The great danger is that the fundamental point will be lost sight of altogether. The mark of the first-class mind as opposed to that of the journeyman or the pedant is that while both must of necessity be led into diversity and detours, the first-class mind always is able to keep the larger object clearly in view, while the lesser intellect ultimatizes minutiae and thrives on infighting.

---

6. Karl Barth, *Church Dogmatics*, III/4, 75.

Not every discipline, if for no other reason than the very uniqueness of the talent necessary to comprehend it, can be expected to make clear to the non-specialist what is going on within it. Such is the case, for instance, with pure mathematics. Other disciplines are, in principle at least, far more accessible to the non-specialist. Indeed, a discipline such as psychology opens itself easily to providing pop psychologies. However, there is nothing inherently contradictory in the doing of psychology as a very elitist enterprise comprehensible only to the *cognoscenti*.

No other discipline, I would imagine, is under quite the same ethical imperative as is Christian theology. For the Christian theologian exists in order to serve the proclamation and the faithful self-understanding of the church. The theologian has a special moral obligation always to stand gladly ready to translate the seeming obscurities of his or her discourse into the ordinary language of non-specialists—the people in the pews. Granted, something may be lost in translation, but something will inevitably be gained as well. Theology cannot be an insular discipline. It serves the preaching and witness of the church. In this, Karl Barth was, I think, totally correct. A theology that cannot be made generally comprehensible in its major foci and fundamental claims, or a theology that fears what will happen if it is understood and withholds the full implication of its intention for fear of unsettling the lay person (in accord with the advice of Paul Tillich), is heretical. As Jesus Christ himself came among us full of grace and truth, so those who witness to him must speak his truth graciously, and graciousness in this context certainly includes comprehensibility and forthrightness.

But does not the ethical and evangelical Christian imperative to clear, definite forthright theological speech stand in unbearable tension with the awful mystery, the eternal otherness of God? How can we, using words created by finite men and women, words that never even remain stable but are constantly relativized by history's constant flow and are further twisted by our self-interests and self-justifications, even remotely hope to speak about a subject holy, invisible, and eternal? It is precisely on this point of the seemingly contradictory requirements to speak boldly and yet to honor the mystery of God by scrupulously avoiding the making of images, graven or verbal, that a great deal of modern and contemporary theological confusion and obfuscation turns. How easy it is to invoke mystery whenever one prefers not to speak—as if mystery can be turned on and off like a spigot. The tension between our evangelical responsibility to speak on the one hand, and the danger of idolatry on the other, cannot be resolved by remaining vague, perhaps hoping that such vagueness will be taken for profundity. The better approach is to recognize the tension and to confront it frankly and explicitly.

We are aided in seeing the overall dimensions of the problem by Thomas Aquinas.[7] Thomas distinguished between three possible ways in which theology might understand its discourse. Theology must understand its language to be univocal, equivocal, or analogical in its intention. Thomas' typology goes directly to the heart of the question of the degree of objective intent that theologians grant to their various theological utterances.

If theology were a purely univocal discourse, then the words it employed in speaking of God would be used in precisely the same way as they are used in ordinary discourse. Thus, an unqualified univocality would render theology an absurdity and even a blasphemy on the face of it. For example, the words, "Our Father, who art in heaven," if univocally understood, would be a petition addressed to a probably gigantic, probably invisible, sexual being who resides beyond the sun, the moon, the planets, and the stars. Thomas well understood that such univocal discourse was a closed option. I know of no theology that would unabashedly conceive of its discourse in this manner, although distressingly, some fundamentalism comes dangerously close.

If such uncomplicated, literal, theological discourse is disallowed at the outset, what about its complete opposite, that is, language that is utterly non-literal and self-repudiating, capable of locating what its object is not, but never what it is? Such is the mode of equivocal discourse. Such discourse typifies the language

---

7. See especially *Summa Theologica*, I, Q. 13, "Names of God."

of many mystics. Since some mysticism is not theistic, such as is the case with Buddhism, one can describe its doctrines under the rubric of "theology" only with qualification. Nonetheless, mystics do characteristically feel the need to point, however guardedly, to the source of their rapture, and thus while some mystics have no "theology" proper, mysticism is generally characterized by concerns that imply at least a religious philosophy. The mystic is willing to live with the paradox that to speak at all distorts the reality discovered in the mystical rapture, for in a real sense nothing can be said of that experience and its meaning; yet, on the other hand, to remain silent is also a distortion, for mere silence would imply that nothing ought to be said. In response to this paradox, discourse can only be an endless series of juxtaposed, mutually exclusive opposites: God does not exist, yet God does not not exist, for example.

The way of equivocation has a long theological history, but it has been—at least until the prominence of Schleiermacher in the nineteenth century and Tillich in the twentieth—the minority view within the Christian theological tradition. Schleiermacher and Tillich, neither of whom were mystics in the classical sense, illustrate that there are grounds other than mysticism on which to base an equivocal understanding of God-talk. Schleiermacher on romantic grounds and Tillich on existentialist grounds both reflected a proclivity for the sort of extra-rational and ontologically ambiguous theological awareness and discourse that has presently become something of a commonplace.

The third and final possibility for understanding the denotative intent of theological language is the way of analogy. Analogical discourse is a discourse that recognizes the impossibility of an across-the-board univocal discourse. It also would avoid the vacuity of thoroughgoing equivocation. Yet analogical discourse entails the recognition that both the impulse to univocality and the impulse to equivocation reflect valid concerns, that is, respectively, the possibility of a true and faithful witness to God and a due awareness of the mystery before which we stand. Therefore, the way of analogy is a genuine attempt to find a middle way.

Analogy focuses on the resemblances, likenesses, or similarities between the attributes, effects, or circumstances of things that, at first glance at least, appear to be entirely different—such as the manifest difference, univocally speaking, between the divine ordering of the cosmos and history on the one hand, and the kingdoms of this world on the other. Yet Jesus spoke of the "kingdom of God." Literally or univocally, the kingdom of God seems an impossible combination of words. Or take the issue of God's interest and involvement in the world, to say nothing of the inner life and being of God as it is equated with the particular human feeling of love. According to 1 John 4:8, "God is love." God is said to be *agape*, disinterested good will, or self-sacrificing love. Literally or univocally, to assert that "God is love" (*agape* or any other species of the passion of affection) raises enormous difficulties. God *is* love? Nevertheless, seen as an analogy and not taken with univocality, the statement "God is love" might well be defended as pointing as far as human understanding and language can take us toward the truth of God's nature and commitment to the creature. To borrow a distinction from E. L. Mascall, "Analogy does not enable us to *conceive* God's goodness [or love or lordship] as identical with his essence, but to *affirm* it as identical with his existence."[8] Obviously, a theology that understands its discourse to be analogical discourse operates out of the ultimate ontological conviction that no matter how great the dissimilarities between God and the creation, there is also sufficient likeness to permit some admittedly imperfect yet somehow valid comparisons.

The great prophets of Israel were radically aware that God's terrible holiness and their own sin rendered them utterly inadequate to speak God's word. In the words of (first) Isaiah, "Woe is me! I am lost, for I am a man of unclean lips, and I live among a people of unclean lips; yet my eyes have seen the King, the Lord of hosts!"[9] Yet at the same time, they were rarely at a loss for words. The prophets had been seized by God's revelation, whether in the

8. *Existence and Analogy*, l20.
9. Isa 6:5.

form of a "burning fire shut up in my bones,"[10] or in a "still small voice,"[11] or in the astonishing visions of Ezekiel.[12] Ezekiel's visions are illustrative of the Old Testament's sense of the dynamic tension between the power and clarity of God's self-disclosure and the great distance that still remains between God and the creature who bears his image. In the midst of his very graphic description of his "visions of God" and of the heavenly court, Ezekiel concludes his recounting of what he has seen with the careful qualification that he saw not God as God is in himself, but rather only "the *appearance of the likeness* of the glory of the Lord."[13] At the very moment of his heightened visual awareness of the very presence of God, Ezekiel saw no contradiction between his vision and God's word to Moses when Moses asked God, "Show me your glory." God replied, "You cannot see my face; for no one shall see me and live."[14] Ezekiel knew that he had seen not God, but only a likeness.

In order to do justice both to the Bible and to mysticism, it is important to emphasize that the Bible is not founded in the experience of mystical rapture. To be sure, there is great passion in the human response to the God of the prophets and apostles. Nevertheless, always in the Bible, the outcome of these passionate encounters between God and the human creature is one of faithful action and speech. The mystic's experience, by contrast, leads to a reticence of speech that is compatible with, if it does not require, quietism. The I-Thou encounter to which the Bible witnesses simply cannot support the quietism that seems to be the consistent logical extension of the *via negativa*.

Thus, for example, Moses at Sinai, as the first order of business, demands and receives God's holy name, without which Moses would have found it impossible to carry out God's holy commission in all its concrete specificity. The very claim that the exodus was

---

10. Jer 20:9.
11. 1 Kgs 19:12.
12. Ezek 1.
13. Ezek 1:1, 28 (emphasis mine).
14. Exod 33:18, 20.

God's will would have been incomprehensible to the Hebrew slaves if Moses had been unable to identify in a polytheistic environment just who this God was.[15] Had Moses experienced an impersonal, ineffable, mystical awareness and not the very personal call and command of Yahweh, a request for God's name would never have occurred to him. But God revealed himself as one who had redemptive goals in the world. Moses knew from the first moment that he who was revealed required of his prophets direct and purposeful speech. Thus Moses even protests that he is a poor public speaker.[16] In the Bible, God is first known in his *effability*.

To be sure, there are but scant hints in the Bible of the denotative status of the Bible's own language. Obviously, the Thomistic distinction between univocal, equivocal, and analogical speech is nowhere to be found. Nevertheless, not a book in the Bible would shrink from the claim that it must of necessity speak of God and that when it does so, it must speak about an unequivocal reality. On the other hand, not a book in the Bible would contradict Paul's ready acknowledgment that "our knowledge is imperfect and our prophecy is imperfect."[17] Thus, it would appear that the Bible, though it does not theorize about the path it will take, in practice travels the middle way between univocality and equivocation—the way of analogy.

Though Thomas' threefold typology is a useful guide for sorting out the possibilities for theological speech, these scholastic modalities have not found universal currency among Protestant theologians. Mascall, writing soon after World War II, found the doctrine widely neglected at that time as well.[18] He held that the tendency of Anglo-Saxon natural theology toward radical immanentism was a function of that neglect. Mascall, however, put the cart before the horse. Analogy is neglected because it points to a way out of immanentism even among those who are fully cognizant of

15. Exod 3:13-17.
16. Exod 4:10.
17. 1 Cor 13:9. Revised Standard Version.
18. Mascall, *Existence and Analogy*, 92ff.

Thomas' typology. There has been nothing like a universal acceptance of this typology even as a point of departure. For example, as has been shown, Tillich preferred to regard theology as a species of symbolic or mythological discourse. Where, one might ask, does Tillich's doctrine of symbols belong in the threefold scholastic typology? Tillich made favorable reference to analogy: the *analogia entis*, and his own *analogia imaginis*. However, he also militantly insisted on the self-negating and, thus it would seem, radically equivocal character of all symbols. Is he therefore best understood as a theologian who functions with a very cautious use of analogy (the more traditionalist reading) or a theologian of equivocation (leading even to an a-theological interpretation of his intentions)? And what of his claim that theology must make at least one literal non-symbolic statement? Thomas' typology, too, is useful in sorting out even so complex and paradoxical a system as Tillich's. In the light of what has been developed in chapter two, it would appear that Tillich is finally a theologian whose ontology must lead to an utterly equivocal theology, but whose Christology and personal faith in Jesus as the Christ drives him at critical moments to an almost univocal, objective affirmation of the historical appearance of the New Being. Thus, one can find him occasionally teaching in terms of "symbols" that are intended to be taken not with his characteristic equivocalness but rather almost as Thomistic analogies. Granted, his characteristic elusiveness makes it nearly impossible ever to be totally confident of anything in these matters; nevertheless, aspects of his understanding of the work of Jesus Christ have a decidedly analogical ring—as it must have, since it is Christian.

There are any number of contemporary theologians who have been influenced by Tillich's doctrine of symbols, but who do not share his Christological commitment. Indeed, many are bent upon a drastic reinterpretation of Christianity that in good old-line liberal fashion would effectively dispense with any recognizable Trinitarianism, the incarnation, divine revelation, and more. It is interesting to see how Tillich's doctrine of symbols, in the hands of his non-Trinitarian contemporary disciples, becomes a tool for subverting Tillich's deepest convictions concerning the authority of

"Jesus as the Christ." Contemporary theology is rife with examples of how the Tillichian doctrine of symbols can be used as a smoke screen behind which to hide thoroughly ontological convictions and as a tool by which to undermine the truth claims of traditional Christianity.

This is illustrated in the doctrines of theological language of two very influential Tillichian, or better, post-Tillichian theologians, Gordon D. Kaufman and Sallie McFague. In spite of their claims to be using radically equivocal symbolic or metaphorical language, both of these thinkers witness against themselves—by their less than forthright but clearly objective theological claims—that it is impossible for theology to be even remotely Christian and actually remain fundamentally equivocal. We saw in the cases of Bultmann and Tillich that a strong Christological commitment necessarily requires that theology finally speak objectively. Kaufman and McFague, whose respective Christologies are rather minimal, illustrate that even theologies that reduce Christianity to ethics cannot avoid "non-symbolic" foundational claims, since ethics deal with the concrete world and therefore must of necessity drag the theology that undergirds it into concrete affirmation.

In his pioneering *Theology for a Nuclear Age*, Kaufman contends that the nuclear age has ushered in a brand new eschatological consciousness. While the eschatology of the Bible envisioned a final destruction, it was to be an extinction presided over by the sovereign God as an expression of his "final triumph over all evil powers"[19] and therefore a destruction with which the godly could live, for the "faithful remnant would survive the catastrophe and, indeed, be glorified. . . ."[20] However, with the advent of the nuclear age, the very obliteration of human life upon the planet earth becomes a possibility, and were it to occur, it would not be God, but "we human beings who are absolutely and fully responsible."[21] Such an event would be "heavy with meaning—and it is all negative" and

---

19. Kaufman, *Theology for a Nuclear Age*, 4.
20. Ibid., 5.
21. Ibid., 7.

with "no redeeming value ... in any of the human intentions and actions that bring this event about."[22] Traditional theology is ill-equipped to deal with this crisis because it either assumes that the sovereign God would not let this happen—a view that Kaufman oddly associates with Karl Barth—or in good fundamentalist fashion supposes that the holocaust could be envisioned as "the ultimate expression of God's sovereignty."[23] This latter view evades our human responsibility and would be "demonically to invoke the divine will as a justification for that very evasion."[24] The former view, trusting in "God's providential care" to keep us from nuclear holocaust, cuts "the nerve of human responsibility," for it assures us that "however horrible nuclear war might be, and however much we are obliged to work against such a calamity, ultimately we can be confident that we humans will not—on our own—be able to bring human history to its end."[25]

Kaufman grants that these two alternatives can be variously "nuanced," and he is unable to deny that such nuanced theological approaches to the nuclear situation have produced "widespread peace and disarmament work by religious groups."[26] Such an admission might seem to stand in tension with Kaufman's claims for his own undertaking, claims made implicit in his rhetorical question: "Why have so few theologians and other religious folk (other than apocalyptic fundamentalists) not been examining, from their special point of view, this momentous religious fact right before our eyes?"[27] His point, I take it, is that while peace movements may abound, they cannot succeed without Kaufman's apparently unprecedented grasp of the "new religious situation," i.e., that nuclear weapons and the "overwhelming and frightening" "*human* power and responsibility" they portend render the

22. Ibid.
23. Ibid., 7–8.
24. Ibid., 8.
25. Ibid.
26. Ibid.
27. Ibid., 5.

traditional theological doctrines of divine sovereignty and an afterlife fatal encumbrances to humanity's solution to the problem.[28] It is clearly Kaufman's implication that only a theology like his will enable Christianity to be positively helpful and not dangerous in defusing the nuclear crisis.

Kaufman developed his theology not long prior to his claim in *Theology for a Nuclear Age* that such a theology is validated and seemingly necessitated by the "momentous religious fact" of nuclear weapons.[29] In such books as *God the Problem* and *The Theological Imagination*, reference to this momentous religious fact is either missing or so tangential that I failed to notice it. Not so astonishingly, in his theological circle this doesn't appear to be a problem. Susan Thistlethwaite in "God and Her Survival in a Nuclear Age" notes that Kaufman's doctrine of God hasn't significantly altered since 1972, yet she can ignore his long theological disregard of the issue and state, "Kaufman is alone in facing this looming catastrophe."[30]

Kaufman's is not an inherently political theology as is Barth's or M. L. King, Jr.'s or Reinhold Niebuhr's. This explains perhaps why he is something of a Johnny-come-lately to theological pondering of nuclear weapons. His insistence on the primacy of the nuclear threat came forty years after Hiroshima. Ironically, Niebuhr, whose theology is closer to Kaufman's than Barth's, and who thus might have been expected to have at least anticipated Kaufman's "breakthrough," in fact had a far less distinguished record on the matter of nuclear weapons as judged from Kaufman's nuclear pacifist perspective than did Barth. Barth, who suffered considerable criticism, not the least from Niebuhr who constantly assaulted Barth's dangerous "neutralism," condemned nuclear weapons *from their inception*, yet worked from the very sort of theology that Kaufman regards as incapable of meeting the situation. It is interesting to note that much of the church leadership of

---

28. Ibid., 8.
29. Ibid., 5.
30. Thistlethwaite, "God and Her Survival," 143–44.

the powerful anti-nuclear movement in Germany throughout the 1980s arose from those who traced their lineage to the Confessing Church in which Barth played such a decisive role.

Though it took two decades of theologizing for Kaufman to discover nuclear weapons, in spite of this hiatus he goes on without apology to charge that the rest of us were largely ignoring them. In a footnote he acknowledges that as early as 1946 some few realized "the religious novelty of the advent of the nuclear age, but their insight seems not to have had much impact on the subsequent theological discussion of the issues at stake."[31] If Kaufman means by this that very few theologians have dared to do their theology in the steady awareness of nuclear weapons to which he has come, then I think self-congratulation has blinded him. If, instead, he is simply saying that few have responded theologically in the Pelagian and Feuerbachian modes of his own approach, he has his point.

In the tragedy of the First World War, Barth saw his beloved liberal theology shattered precisely because many of his teachers believed their liberalism justified that catastrophic war. Thus, Barth was determined to start over theologically. There is, I think, a difference between this sequence of events and the situation of having a theology already established and using tragedy—as in the case of Kaufman and nuclear weapons—as a way to hawk one theological perspective. It is one thing for an individual to be driven to his stance by the impact of evil on a position he has held and can hold no longer, and thus, with sorrow and regret, to be compelled to criticize first himself for having believed and cherished such a view, and only secondarily to criticize others. It is quite another thing to use the problem of evil as a club with which to beat one's theological opponents. Does Kaufman's Pelagianism extend to the point of naïvely supposing that he is immune to the problem of evil? The problem of evil is a two-edged sword that inevitably strikes the theologian who would wield it as surely as it strikes his opponents.

---

31. Kaufman, *Theology for a Nuclear Age*, 15 n. 9.

If as the result of nuclear weapons "the personalistic conception of God, so powerfully presented by the traditional images of Christian and Jewish piety, seems less and less defensible," are we unfair to anticipate a theology as unprecedented as is our new situation itself?[32] What does Kaufman provide? A rehash of left-wing Protestant liberalism; to wit, theology is an "imaginative construction"; God is therefore "the ultimate point of reference for all understanding of anything; by 'God' we mean the ultimate object of devotion for human life."[33] Feuerbach said as much before the advent of the tank, to say nothing of the bomb. Kaufman insists that the Bible and the tradition of the church have no binding authority. They are merely the source and repository of the symbols with which the contemporary Western theologian must work. In seemingly good Tillichian fashion, Kaufman claims that all such concepts and images are only "analogies or metaphors, symbols or models, drawn from human experience" and never to be taken literally or univocally.[34] Literal use of these symbols is idolatry. Presumably other religions with their symbols, images, and concepts are not lesser systems merely because their symbols are not the Western theologian's prime focus, i.e., God and Jesus Christ. The specific symbols in any religion, it would appear, are not themselves as important as that which the theologian finds of value in them in his or her reconstructive undertaking. Thus, "a central task of theology is to become aware of the various metaphors, images, and models which have been and can be used for putting together this symbol [the symbol of God] and to develop criteria for choosing among them."[35] In short, over the whole religious enterprise stands the scrutinizing theologian as he or she imperiously sorts out the components of the symbol for God. The authority of Scripture and tradition has been utterly rejected in order that the authority of the theologian as the creator and critic of the symbol of God may have full reign.

32. Ibid., 9.
33. Ibid., 21 and passim., 25.
34. Ibid., 25.
35. Ibid., 26.

And the criteria by which theology's critical judgments are made?

> A supreme test, one might say, of the ultimate viability, and thus finality of the truth, of the Christian symbols—or of any other symbolic frame of orientation for human life, for that matter—is their capacity to provide insight and guidance in our situation today, a situation in which humankind has come up against its own limits in the most decisive and paradoxical way: through gaining the power utterly to obliterate itself.[36]

Kaufman's theology presumably passes muster better at least than all those he criticizes, although in the book there are occasional obligatory gestures toward humility in his routine recognition that he doesn't have all the answers. Indeed, *Theology for a Nuclear Age* concludes with a rather banal plea for human unity in the work that lies before us all. Theology can't do it alone. But humanity united can save itself. Such a salvation is the only salvation Kaufman recognizes.

Kaufman's unrelenting reference to symbol, particularly in light of his reference to Tillilch's paradoxical adage, "God is a symbol for God,"[37] gives the superficial impression that he may be serving up something of the same rich—if maddening—theological stew that Tillich himself prepared in his doctrine of symbols. However, in comparison to Tillich, Kaufman's symbolic doctrine of God is quite straightforward in its almost literal and, again, banal reduction of theology to an uncomplicated and unambiguous naturalistic, Pelagian anthropocentrism: "The proper criterion for our talk about God . . . is not the postulation of some being or reality beyond the world but rather concern with the relativizing and humanizing activity going on within the world."[38]

In the nuclear age God is no longer a transcendent "quasi-person" for whom "anthropomorphic images" such as lord or parent are appropriate. Rather, "God should today be conceived in

---

36. Ibid., 28.
37. Kaufman, *God the Problem*, 82.
38. Kaufman, *Theology in a Nuclear Age*, 37.

terms of the complex of physical, biological, and historico-cultural conditions that have made human existence possible, which continue to sustain it, and which may draw it out to fuller humanity and humanness."[39] God is the "whole grand cosmic evolutionary movement" as it gives birth to "*us*" in our "finite freedom and self-consciousness in and through our human history...."[40] Therefore, God's agenda is enlightened humanity's agenda, so that presumably the nuclear extinction of the planet would signal the demise of God as well as humanity. Our fate on earth has become God's fate.[41] What Kaufman is calling for in practical, ethical terms is the liberal social, political, ecological agenda brought to bear against the threat of nuclear weapons.

As one who, after having pondered nuclear weapons for years, has *never* even remotely considered that a nuclear holocaust would be a theologically salutary phenomenon, I can salute Kaufman's goals, but so can every liberal atheist in the world as well. Why would we need God-talk to convey the message to rational human beings, be they religious or irreligious, who have a clearly vested interest in the matter, that humankind is worth preserving, and that if we destroy the ecosystem by the use of nuclear weapons (or global warming, for that matter), everyone dies, and that therefore we ought to galvanize our intelligence and energy to avert these catastrophes. Neither ethically nor practically is Kaufman telling the atheist anything he or she doesn't already know. And I would imagine that many atheists in politics and science who have a technical grasp of the terribly complicated nuts and bolts of nuclear disarmament might be as much irritated as edified by the pious platitudes of theologians about the evils of nuclear annihilation.

Yet Kaufman's most egregious heresy is not his lamentable confusion of the nouns "God" and "humanity," nor is it his rank Pelagianism; it lies in the fact that by reducing theology to anthropology, since every conceivable aspect of human existence is

39. Ibid., 42.
40. Ibid., 44.
41. Ibid., 45.

already staked out by philosophy and the sciences, physical and social, he is coming dangerously close to putting theologians out of a job. Why would anyone need theology any longer once it is admitted that its only subject is humanity?

Kaufman's answer to such a question is clearly not that we need theology because the God of Israel exists as the Lord of the universe and we his creatures *must,* because we are his creatures, even creatures in rebellion, take account of his lordship since he is taking account of our creatureliness by his faithful sustaining of the universe. Kaufman would regard this as a false and dangerous idea that assumes that God in his sovereign providence and electing will is our ever-present help in time of trouble. God's rod and his staff are no comfort to Kaufman. For Kaufman, to put it crudely, God himself is helped by those who help themselves. We are solely responsible for the ongoing history of the world. If we don't save it nobody will. Potential nuclear and ecological catastrophe symbolize for us "the stark fact of total human responsibility for the earthly future of humanity...."[42]

Therefore, in spite of the fact that for Kaufman the transcendent personal God of the Bible and Christian traditions does not exist, there may still be a need for "Christian" theologians after all, for theologians are still the prime intellectual exponents of the symbol "God." And there's life in the old symbol yet. "'God,' as no other name or concept in our Western languages, holds together in a unity that complex reality which grounds and sustains our human existence...."[43] Thus, the West still needs the counsel that the Christian theologian can give as it seeks the unity that alone can save humanity from nuclear catastrophe. Kaufman believes that the present nuclear crisis requires that we elevate the doctrine of the suffering of God in Jesus Christ—so powerfully witnessed to in the New Testament—to a position of absolute primacy. The cross of Jesus Christ alone becomes the sole legitimate symbol of God's relation to the world. For God exercises no power to redeem us or

42. Ibid., 8.
43. Ibid., 42–43.

his Son. Redemption is in our hands. The doctrine of the resurrection is, thus, a false reversion to a divine triumphalism: "The symbolism of cross and resurrection by Christians not only drew the sting from the motif of absolute self-sacrifice by transforming it into a kind of ultimate prudence and self-aggrandizement; it also laid the foundations for later Christian imperialism."[44]

It is true enough that faith in the resurrection can be perverted into a justification of imperialism. Surely Kaufman does not mean to suggest that imperialism is somehow the *inevitable* result of such a faith. The Marxists' claim that faith in eternal life can be used as an opiate seems to point to a different danger. In fact, both imperialism and passivity are distorted responses to the event of Christ's resurrection. Nothing that God does unto the human race, no matter how gracious his gifts, is immune to human distortion. But it would be a terrible distortion of the record to suppose that the only fruit of resurrection faith historically has been imperialism or social passivity.

On the other hand, a denial of eternal life need not lead to a life of worldly virtue and beneficence. Neither the social Darwinists, nor Hitler, nor for that matter the "me" generation saw any connection between this-worldly naturalism and a life of self-giving love. For many, if this life is all they have, why should they waste it on the weak? Why sacrifice even a moment of one's fleeting existence? Kaufman's charges respecting eternal life cut both ways. Even among those Christians who deny the resurrection, this denial is no sure-fire guarantee of attaining to the humility of Christ. If the resurrection and the triumph of God's righteousness are species of prudential self-aggrandizement, can we not detect at least a little pomposity and vacuousness in a tenured, Ivy-League professor wrapping himself in the mantle of the "motif of absolute self-sacrifice?" Do I fail to understand the term "self-aggrandizement"? Or is it not lurking in the following:

> It must be acknowledged immediately that this understanding of salvation cannot appeal directly to motives of self-interest;

44. Ibid., 50.

> neither a peaceful and contented life on earth, nor eternal bliss in heaven is its expected reward. On the contrary, radical self-giving in struggle with the worst evils of contemporary human life, culminating perhaps in a complete self-sacrifice—crucifixion—is what is to be expected. The only reward promised here is the consciousness that one is expending one's life and energy to help liberate men and women from the evils which presently enslave them; one is seeking to help make future human life more humane and fulfilling than life today; one is giving up oneself for others.[45]

Further, how can a theology whose validation is measured by its capacity to assure the survival of the human species claim to be free of "motives of self-interest"?

I hope that my comments make it clear that I find Kaufman's theology a less than intriguing bit of old-line liberal reductionism—reducing Christianity to the simple deification of the human struggle to survive against the products of its own hands. And as such I find it a breathtaking example of species chauvinism equal in conceit, if not in originality, to Feuerbach's own anthropocentric self-adulation.

Kaufman's claims for the practical historical implications of his theology are tangential to the issue at hand, which is the inevitability of the objective-analogical implication in all theology. Nevertheless, it is hard to resist observing that from a purely historical point of view, the triumph of an immanental theology of a deified humanity seems less the answer to the impending catastrophe that Kaufman portends but far more its cause. Could Kaufman have somehow overlooked that the contemporary theology of the immanental deification of humanity has been the chief and culturally dominant rival of biblical Christianity for the hearts and minds of Western intellectuals since the Enlightenment and before? And that it is under the sway of such a God that we have witnessed such tyrannies as Hitler and Stalin? Or that it was out of a terror before the prospect that Hitler would get nuclear weapons first that even so commendable an immanentist theist as Albert Einstein advocated their construction?

45. Ibid., 59.

Kaufman, like all Pelagians, seems utterly impervious to the ironies of history. If historical events could lead such a man as Albert Einstein to advocate the building of nuclear weapons, how can Kaufman be so naïve as to imagine that by marshaling of the world's religious and technical expertise toward the Kaufmanesque vision of "salvation," we can take sufficient control of events so as to free ourselves from the "cunning" of history? If Kaufman, in spite of the track record of a self-deified humanity, thinks we need to stand fast in such self-deification, let him make his case. But surely, on the track record of his god, rational people will not mistake it for the Prince of Peace.

But to the central issue, Kaufman's use of religious language and his adaptation of the Tillichian concept of symbol serve primarily two functions in his theology. The concept "symbol" is used as a tool for tearing down biblical and traditional understandings of the being and doings of God by relativizing them as mere symbols. But his doctrine of symbol also provides Kaufman with what I take to be a smoke screen behind which he can set up his idol—humanity itself.

At one level the supposition that all religious language is "symbolic" carries with it the implication that theology is not only utterly culturally relative—a cluster of finally arbitrary cultural images—but that theology is and must be radically pliable—subject to constant and deliberate alteration as its historical context changes. Therefore, the theologian, as the imaginative constructor of symbols and diviner of their meaning and significance, has utterly free rein. Tillich's own reverence for the way in which symbols are born and die independent of our intention seems largely lacking under Kaufman's strong right arm. Symbols can be created and discarded according to the passing requirements of Kaufman's reading of the significance of the historical moment. Beyond this, Kaufman has little or no sense of a symbol or Bible passage calling him up short. In good Marcionite fashion, the symbols he doesn't like are rejected out of hand. For Kaufman, their value or danger are judged purely by their utilitarian capacity either to aid or undermine humanity's attempt to save itself. They appear to have no other truth or falsity.

At first glance, since he claims that his own imaginative reconstructions of Christian symbols are themselves symbolic, it would appear that he is modestly claiming no more for his own discourse than he grants to his traditionalist foes. But of course this is not the case. For example, Kaufman believes quite literally that there exists no personal or objective God, that there is no human survival after the grave, and that the mysterious side of God's nature lies in the mystery of the wholly immanental evolving cosmos. Therefore, devotion to God means devotion to life and above all to human life, as human life alone is capable of assessing the worth of life. The clear "ultimate concern" in all this need not be, indeed it cannot be, expressed symbolically. Kaufman's ultimate concern is the quite literal, unequivocal deliverance of the human race from nuclear annihilation.

What Kaufman's theology thus illustrates is that no Christian theology avoids the implication at one point or another of objective, even unequivocal ultimate claims. Perhaps a pure, totally non-ethical mysticism (if such existed) could theoretically avoid this implication. Suppose there were a mysticism that conceived itself in terms of an utter quietism—totally centered in the experience of mystical rapture itself. Sublimely and ethically indifferent to whether other people know or do not know of this rapture, such a mystic could avoid all discourse objective or equivocal—the only unequivocal reality being that the mystic *had* an experience. No mystic I have ever heard of would quite fit such a non-ethical, utterly privatized model. The mystics I know generally choose to speak.

My point is that Christianity, in order for it to be Christianity, be it a Christianity of the right or the left, must of necessity have an ethical, communal dimension. However, insofar as one's theology has this inevitable ethical dimension it cannot merely equivocate, even if it may elsewhere claim to embrace the *via negativa*. For if theology carries with it any ethical authority at all, it is saying, in effect, that this or that concrete act is more or less consistent with the being of the highest reality, while some other act is not. Indeed, no ethic is defensible if it stands by itself without a larger theological, metaphysical, or ontological basis. James Gustafson, one "liberal" ethicist who can never be accused of ontological evasiveness, has made this clear in many contexts over many years.[46] To refuse to admit at least *this* non-equivocal foundation in one's theology is to deny that one's theology has any ethical consequence whatsoever.

We can see in a somewhat different form the same inability to keep equivocal theological discourse stable in the theology of Sallie McFague in her *Models of God: Theology for an Ecological, Nuclear Age*. As her title suggests, McFague is influenced by Kaufman, but hers is a somewhat more elusive doctrine of theological discourse than is his.

In an attempt to clear out space for her own theology, though doing some considerable injustice to the rich symbolic subtlety of the work of Schleiermacher and Tillich, while apparently overlooking the wooden literalism of Kaufman's construction, McFague lumps Schleiermacher and Tillich together with Kaufman as being "basically constructive" theologians. For her own part, she sees her own "metaphorical," constructive theology as being more characterized by the adjectives "'experimental,' "pluralistic," and "imagistic," than what she styles the "'systematic,' "comprehensive," "conceptual" stance of the other three.[47]

Though her preferred adjectives would suggest an even greater elusiveness *vis-à-vis* the Christian tradition than theologians who are systematic, comprehensive, and conceptual, McFague in places gives the appearance of being closer to the tradition than they. For example, her claim that God is personal would seem to take her far closer to biblical Christianity than to Schleiermacher, Tillich, or Kaufman—all of whom deny the fact.

> ... [I]t seems to me that to be a Christian is to be persuaded that there is a personal, gracious power who is on the side of life and fulfillment, a power whom the paradigmatic figure Jesus of Nazareth expresses and illuminates, but when we try to say

---

46. See his *Ethics from a Theocentric Perspective*.
47. McFague, *Models of God*, 37, 196 n. 14.

> something more, we turn, necessarily, to the "loves" we know (unless one is a Barthian and believes that God defines love and that all human love only conforms to the divine pattern).[48]

Such affirmations notwithstanding, in the end McFague stands in the tradition of classical liberalism, a perspective that is inevitably ambiguous regarding the God of Israel, for as Colin E. Gunton so aptly observed, liberalism is "anchored in that tradition of Western philosophy which regards philosophic abstractions as intellectually more respectable than the allegedly cruder anthropomorphisms of biblical origin."[49] His comment, though directed to Charles Hartshorne's theology, holds true for liberalism.

While McFague wants to hold on to *talk* about a "personal, gracious" God, it remains unclear if such sentiments are any more than a sentimental residue. For what she finally holds out for does not appear to be a personal God at all, but rather anthropomorphism as a useful "model" for illustrating a more basic and prior conviction, i.e., "the initial assumption or belief . . . that God is on the side of life and its fulfillment."[50] It must be noted that there is a radical difference between a theology that begins in an abstract "initial assumption" and one that begins in the existential experience of a personal God. In the Bible, faith begins in an I-Thou encounter, and thus the personhood of God is the first and most basic fact to which faith bears witness. However, the most that McFague claims for faith in a personal God is that such language serves to "*project a possibility.*"[51] Indeed, McFague is, in the end, entirely agnostic concerning the question as to whether her "models of God" as personal, i.e., as "mother, lover, and friend," are in any sense reflections of the inner life of God. McFague takes as basic the claim that no one can ever know—certainly not in this life, and since McFague rejects the Christian faith in life beyond the

---

48. Ibid., 192 n. 37.
49. Gunton, *Becoming and Being*, 221.
50. McFague, *Models of God*, 192 n. 37.
51. Ibid. (Emphasis in original.)

grave[52] she also must reject out of hand anything like John Hick's argument for an eschatological verification of our God-talk. Thus, what could theology ever be but irresolvable projections?

McFague holds that the utter tentativeness of such theological modeling distinguishes hers, as a metaphorical theology, from more traditional, analogical theologies.[53] In her definitional framework, she appears to see analogy as entailing a stronger claim than does metaphor. The distinction she draws is, I think, misleading. For after all, metaphors and analogies do much the same work, although metaphor generally does that work in a more obviously figurative manner. As far back as Thomas Aquinas, for example, there is theological precedent for using the two terms virtually synonymously.

Every metaphor or analogy tries to illuminate some reality or insight, yet every metaphor or analogy is literally false. "God is our heavenly Father" is an attempt to say something about the nature of God's relationship to humanity. Of course, one might argue that it is an inept or oppressive analogy, as some feminists do, but even the argument that it is a bad analogy assumes that the goal of analogy is to shed light upon *some* truth—for if there is no assumption of *some* truth there are no criteria to argue for or against the appropriateness of any analogy over any other. Clearly McFague sees some models as better than others.

On the other hand, every analogy or metaphor is on the face of it literally false. Our heavenly Father is not a man beyond the sky. Therefore, while it is the case that analogy or metaphor can be intended as Thomas Aquinas intended them, that is, to point toward God as *far as they go*, it is also the case that since they are also literally false, they can be put to an opposite service. While they can be tools of traditional theological discourse, they can also be employed in the service of the most radical *via negativa*. That is, they can be used to stress the falseness of all literal discourse

---

52. Ibid., 60.
53. Ibid., 192 n. 37.

and by extension the alleged indefensibility of analogy itself. Since Tillich, much theology has equivocated on this issue.

Once one sees that the real question is not metaphor versus analogy, but in Thomas' terms, "pure equivocation" versus analogy (in which "names" that signify the divine substance are predicated substantially of God although they fall short of a full representation of him), then we can begin to separate those doctrines.[54] We can unpack McFague's ontologically ambiguous, equivocal program of metaphorical modeling and those doctrines that she, somewhat less than frankly, but nevertheless firmly and ontologically, affirms by analogy.

In order to give the impression of doing a theology that makes only tentative, fragile claims, McFague's theology is replete with seemingly modest disclaimers. She frankly admits, for example, that she is caught in "something of a circular argument" from which she can find no escape:

> I do not *know* who God is, but I find some models better than others for constructing an image of God commensurate with my trust in a God as on the side of life. God is and remains a mystery. We really do not know: the hints and clues we do have of the way things are—whether we call them experiences, revelation, or whatever—are too fragile, too little (and more often than not, too negative) for much more than a hypothesis, a guess, a projection of a possibility that, although it can be comprehensive and illuminating, may not be true. We can believe it is and act as if it were, but it is, to use Ricoeur's term, a "wager." [Was it not Pascal's term first?] At the most, I find I can make what Philip Wheelwright calls a "shy ontological claim...."[55]

In a discussion of the implications of her "shy" ontology for the question of the existence of God, McFague argues that "something is there," but it can be described only metaphorically, for "we do not know how to talk about it."[56]

---

54. *Summa Theologica*, I, Q. 13, Art. 5.
55. *Models of God*, 192f. n. 37.
56. Ibid., 196 n. 13.

However, there also are passages in which McFague suggests an almost perfect dovetailing of her methodology with its object. Thus, the metaphorical character of theological discourse (i.e., the *via negativa* with a boost from deconstructionism) would seem to be itself a virtual revelation of its object. As the language of faith is fundamentally equivocal, so too is the very ontological reality of God. Therefore, "God both 'is' and 'is not.'" The way we speak of God, i.e., equivocally, reveals a certain "notness" in the heart of God, in spite of the "presumptuous" fact that Western religion is loath to teach this. "God *is not*, not just in the sense of being unavailable to us or absent from our experience but as a basic aspect of the being of God."[57]

Though this sounds like an explicitly ontological utterance to me, there is a further disclaimer: "To affirm all this, however, does not mean there is not a reality (nor does it mean that there is)...."[58] This theology is perhaps not so much shy as it is coy. McFague modestly concludes her work with the soft claim that "it is mostly fiction, mainly fleshing out a few basic metaphors"[59]—metaphors that are destabilizing, inclusive, and non-hierarchical.

I must admit that my reaction to this and all the other bits of self-deprecating modesty with which her work is studded is that they are counterfeit. It is rather like the modesty of the coquette who exhibits a demeanor seemingly attractive, unassuming, and yielding but behind which lies a whole arsenal of passive-aggressive drives and finally an agenda as inflexible as any of the "orthodoxy" that she rejects.

In her attempt to make limited use of and thus to domesticate the deconstructionist movement, McFague reveals, I think, more then she might wish. For here, curiously, we can see something of just how and why she really believes that her theology is ontologically right—at least compared to anyone else's. Thus, while she is critical of deconstructionism's denial that there is any truth outside

57. Ibid.
58. Ibid.
59. Ibid., 182.

of texts themselves, she finds deconstructionism to be useful in exposing those dogmatists whose "safe havens, called dogmas and orthodoxy, become absolutes, giving the illusion of being certain, being 'on the inside,' having the truth."[60] McFague is surprisingly naïve in supposing that deconstructionism can be turned into an handy weapon with which contemporary inheritors of old-line liberalism can bash their "orthodox" foes, but never be bashed themselves—leaving aside the fact that none of the great theologians but only perhaps their most slavish followers were ever orthodox in the lockstep manner McFague parodies.

Deconstructionism teaches us to "endure absence, uncertainty, partiality, relativity and to hold at bay the desire for closure, coherence, identity, totality."[61] But we could have learned what is valid in all this from the "orthodox" Augustine.[62] Augustine shared much of deconstructionism's anxiety over the attempt to put the truth into words; however, Augustine *qua* rhetorician turned theologian, profoundly and with great originality ruminated in a spirit anything but nihilistic over the nearly insoluble problems surrounding the inadequacy of our language and our understanding. Augustine came to his recognition of the indeterminacy of our language not as an atheist, but from a theocentric posture. Barth (whose theology McFague seems to despise), from an Augustinian theocentric perspective, radically anticipated deconstructionism's horror of any claim being able to encapsulate the truth. Therefore, it is wholly illegitimate to employ nihilistic deconstructionism as a tool for doing in the whole Augustinian deconstructionist tradition—that is, unless one is willing to subject oneself to the full array of its nihilistic strictures.

McFague is saying, in essence, that deconstructionism is perfectly correct in calling the turn on all the claims that "traditional" theology wishes to privilege, but not the claims that I, McFague, wish to privilege. Of course, McFague has no book if she does

---

60. Ibid., 25.
61. Ibid., 25f.
62. See, e.g., Augustine, *Trinity* and *On Christian Teaching*.

not break with deconstructionism's utter relativism and denial of anything "outside language." For if deconstructionism were right about this, then the upshot must be that McFague's own models are no better or worse than the models she criticizes. This she does not believe for a moment. Taking a leaf from Kaufman, she makes it clear that she believes that world survival itself may be tied up in her "critique of the triumphalist, imperialistic, patriarchical model" and its replacement by such models as "mother, lover, friend."[63] McFague may not know much for certain about God. Her theology, she writes, is "in the tradition of the *via negativa*: finding little to say of God with certainty, it boldly makes its case hypothetically and lets it rest."[64] However, she clearly knows what sorts of metaphors and models will permit us to "remythologize Christian faith" in a manner "appropriate for an ecological, nuclear age."[65] I simply do not see how she could know so much—nothing less than the general lines along which to "remythologize" the whole of Christianity as well as what is "appropriate" to the needs of the modern world, if she didn't believe that she knew a good deal more about God and the truth of the human situation than she lets on.

Those traditional Christians who assert that God is the lone, self-existent sovereign Lord of the universe do so presumably because their experience of God is consistent with the biblical tradition. If God is who believers standing in this tradition testify that he has revealed himself to be, then McFague's rejection of all metaphors of sovereign lordship is a willful attempt to supplant the traditional Christian God with a god of her own invention.

McFague however, writes as one who has no concerns on this score. She could not so confidently assert that traditional language about divine lordship and dominion is inappropriate for our time unless she believed that it was also, finally, ontologically wrong. To build one's whole theology out of the radical claim that the Western tradition is dangerous is only coherent if one also assumes

63. McFague, *Models of God*, 20.
64. Ibid., 40.
65. Ibid.

it is also fundamentally wrong, which of course it may indeed be. But once one acknowledges the possibility of even relative—to say nothing of fundamental—error, only one who is thoroughly deranged would speak absent the confidence that one's alternative model is at least *less* wrong. There is really no way one can escape the implication of having a full-blown theological agenda, if not overt then hidden, once one criticizes others.

In a very revealing bit of modesty, McFague states, "[T]he project as such, this kind of theology as a whole, is a tentative affair and can advance few solid claims in its own behalf."[66] The word "few," I think, gives the game away. How can her theology of hypothetical models make *any* solid claims, to say nothing of a few? The whole question of a totally self-repudiating symbol system examined in the chapter on Tillich rears its head. If she had said that her theology can advance *no* solid claims, one could hardly fault the sincerity of her shyness and theological modesty. However, a theology claiming no tie whatsoever to the truth of things would have no basis whatsoever to make an appeal to human ethical action. Why should one act on the basis of a religion that gives up the attempt to find the truth? Christianity inevitably must attempt to speak the truth about God and God's relationship and relevance to the world if it is to speak comprehensibly, not to say persuasively, to the world.

A theology that wants to insulate itself from the onslaught of skepticism or wishes to make itself virtually invulnerable to the attacks of other theologians can always hide behind claims of the tenuousness of its assertions. Again, as McFague would style her theology, "It boldly makes its case hypothetically and lets it rest."[67] This all but ends the argument. One can hardly expect a dispute from someone so boldly at rest. However, what one gains in the invulnerability of one's claims, so shyly offered, one loses in ethical or any other kind of human relevance. If we are merely discussing someone's "bold" hypotheses as those hypotheses are held in the

66. Ibid.
67. Ibid.

air by their own bootstraps, how can such a theology be compelling to the general run of humanity? This is especially urgent in McFague's case, for if the claims she makes for her theology are correct, humanity needs her sort of "open, caring, inclusive, interdependent, changing, mutual and creative" perspective if it is to save itself from catastrophe.[68] It is the last great hope of the nuclear age. Yet we need not fear on this score. Those "few solid claims" that Mcfague does make for her theology, first appearances aside, are so sweeping and dogmatically definitive that we need not be concerned that *her* theology will be left hanging in the air. As has been observed with Tillich, a systematic theology needs not a few but only one objective statement to save itself from airy circularity. Surely McFague is offering precisely such a statement under the guise of what she calls an "experiment."

> What this experiment with the world as God's body comes to finally, is an awareness, both chilling and breathtaking, that we as worldly, bodily beings are in God's presence. It is the basis for a revived sacramentalism, that is, a perception of the divine as visible, as present, palpably present in our world. . . . We meet the world as a Thou, as the body of God where God is present to us always in all times and in all places.[69]

Despite the pantheistic ring of the above, McFague's overall theology is better described as a species of panentheism—hers being an old-line romantic version of the same. For McFague, God is not simply the world, God is rather in some sense the mytho-poetically conceived personal essence of the world whose transcendence is comprised of the fact that immanence does not exhaust "her" reality. In order to describe how it is that this God, who is the body of the world, can also transcend the world, McFague refers to our passionate feelings in our response to the world both in its telescopic grandeur and in its microscopic intricacy. For both the experience of the very large and the very small elicits from us, as sensitive viewers, a feeling of profound awe and wonder. McFague

---

68. Ibid., 13.
69. Ibid., 77.

claims that such awe and wonder correspond to what earlier theologians were getting at when they described the attributes of the transcendent God abstractly, that is, in terms of "infinity, eternality, omniscience, omnipresence, and so forth."[70] One might have thought they had something more in mind.

In justifying the fact that she has so little to say about the transcendence of God, McFague lets slip the admission that the metaphors that would comprise a remythologized expression of our "feeling of awe, reverence [and] wonder" are "as yet unknown and unplumbed metaphors."[71] Thus, she implicitly acknowledges what the positive tone of her discourse in these matters would seem to require; that is to say, when she locates what "traditional" theology calls "transcendence" in our human feeling for the richness of the world that we experience prior to any metaphorical modeling she is at that point not speaking metaphorically at all. Thus, in the final analysis, after all the tentative, experimental, fresh new modeling of God in seemingly shy, non-dogmatic terms, we come to recognize that such language does have a final referent, a referent that McFague believes objectively: God is our awareness of our relationship to aspects of the world. While eschewing hard ontological convictions, McFague rather disingenuously ends up in a literalization of the Schleiermachian claim that God is the "feeling of absolute dependence," or as McFague would prefer, the feeling of awe and wonder before the world.

A well-nigh universal move made in all such revisionist theologies, be they constructive, deconstructive, nuclear, ecological, feminist, etc., is the insistence that the whole structure of Christian theology is but a historically relative (if still interesting) expression of a universal human religious impulse. The impulse itself being, of course, variously represented in various religions, or denominations, or theological schools. The problem for such theologians is therefore how to keep one's own theology from being relativized into the same limbo where one has cast everyone else's. The trick in

---

70. Ibid., 186.
71. Ibid.

all this is to keep one's own convictions hidden behind the smoke screen afforded by the doctrine that all theology is equivocally metaphorical or symbolic. The attempt has been made to illustrate what a sleight of hand this finally is. Insofar as any theology intends be in *any* way relevant to the world it must at least assume hard ontological assumptions. Upon analysis, no matter how shy, coy, symbolic, or metaphorical a theology may style itself, every theology's ontological hand can be forced. The cases of Kaufman and McFague amply illustrate this claim.

Some considerable care has been taken to examine Kaufman and McFague's use of their doctrines of symbol or metaphor because they epitomize the revisionist reductionism that has typified the wing of American academic theology that is still traditionalist enough to try to make some positive use of the "symbol," God.

As has been shown, Paul Tillich, though he did not satisfy it, seemed to understand the necessity for theology's making at least one non-symbolic statement about God. Of course, this does not mean that an across-the-board non-symbolic discourse is even remotely possible. However, at some point, theology must indicate what its symbols, metaphors, tropes, and analogies are finally all about. Kaufman and McFague's respective judgments concerning the relative inadequacy of "traditional" symbols or metaphors and the relative greater adequacy of their own symbolic and metaphorical constructions finally have no more claim to serious theological attention than do their various color preferences. Even their pragmatic claims that only a new theology can be serviceable in saving humanity from self-destruction rests on the assumption that it is objectively true that human beings do better when they are answerable to no sovereignty; and that it is in our power to reshape according to our needs the character and scope of divine authority. If we were to grant to such revisionism just such exceptions to its otherwise blanket claim that theology is finally indeterminate metaphor, then of course it can go on with ruthless consistency on the question of the mytho-poetic nature of theological discourse and thereby relativize every theological claim—save for its own *sub rosa* preserves of ultimacy.

It is ironic that in the early writings of Barth—nineteenth-century theological liberalism's most incisive and influential critic and thus the chief object of the odium of contemporary revisionist neo-liberal theology—we should find a view of theological language that is so radically equivocal that it seems almost the flip side of the contemporary philosophical and theological preoccupation with metaphors and indeterminacy. The difference is that Barth believed that his dialectical and indeterminate language of paradox and crisis was the only way to witness to the radical transcendence and eternal sovereignty of God, whereas revisionist theologians claim that indeterminate, metaphorical discourse is the only way to witness the utter immanence or even the very interment of God. Barth's "dialectical theology," particularly as it was expressed in the second edition of his *Epistle to the Romans* (1922),[72] was characterized by the contention that every theological statement contained an error, which must be corrected by another statement that also contained an error, which in turn must be corrected by another theological statement, *ad infinitum*. Barth, influenced by Kierkegaard's insistence on the either-or character of the Christian faith, intended a deliberate contrast to Hegel's dialectic in which truth was conceived of as a both-and proposition. For Hegel, in the history of thought, every prevailing idea that is the thesis of each era generates its opposite idea, the antithesis, and out of the conflict of the thesis and the antithesis there results a synthesis; that is, a higher idea that incorporates something of the thesis and something of the antithesis to produce a progressively higher insight than could be found in either by themselves. Barth insisted that indeed there was, in theological discourse, a dialectic of thesis and antithesis. However, the synthesis could never be humanly achieved. Only the broken insight, endlessly needing to be corrected by another broken insight, was theologically possible.

In his influential book on Barth, the Roman Catholic Hans Urs von Balthasar argues that the 1922 *Epistle to the Romans*, written in Barth's most extreme dialectical mood, created a fundamental

---

72. The first edition of *Epistle to the Romans* was published in 1919.

contradiction.[73] In opposition to the virtually univocal anthropocentricism of liberalism that Feuerbach so caustically exposed as the self-evident proof of the root of the actual atheism implicit in theological liberalism, Barth set out to speak about the holy lordship of the transcendent and sovereign God. Nevertheless, Barth, in insisting that all theological language is held in the grip of his drastic dialectic, undid his own best intentions. According to von Balthasar, Barth's dialectical method "actually betrays its mission to speak only of God and focuses attention on itself instead. In protesting its limitations, it turns them into absolutes."[74] What is deconstructionism but the turning of language limitations into absolutes? Barth himself became aware of the problem. Indeed, Barth became the popularizer of his own long-standing rejection of the dialectical extremes of the *Epistle to the Romans* in his widely read *Humanity of God*.[75] As he made his slow and painful way from existentialism, it became abundantly clear that Barth had never intended his theology as a modern *via negativa*. As Barth began to recognize the subjective and reductionist implications of his existentialist dialectics, he turned from his early work as a mere marginal corrective to liberalism to the positive task of dogmatics of doctrine. Even though Barth himself was slow to see it, it was always his intention to point in an objective, doctrinal manner to God. Nevertheless, Barth's critics in the early 1920s were not completely without foundation in reading him as a strange new mystic or the founder of a cult. Nor should we forget that Barth's radical dialectical method provided a means by which twentieth-century neo-liberalism could weather Barth's onslaught against liberalism and turn back to a chastened and thus strengthened liberalism as if nothing had happened. Thus, it is not to be forgotten that Tillich, in spite of this antipathy to Barth's book with its turn toward what he regarded as orthodoxy, always regarded the dialectical theology

73. Balthasar, *Theology of Karl Barth*.

74. Ibid., 72.

75. Originally delivered as a lecture in 1956. See Barth, *Humanity of God*, 37ff.

of the 1922 *Epistle to the Romans* as a kind of theological revelation. Barth's dialectical method could also be read as a first shot in Bultmann's existentialist demythologization program. Even Barth was surprised (pleasantly at the time) that Bultmann, rooted as he was in liberalism, spoke so positively of Barth's 1922 anti-liberal bombshell. Bultmann, the existentialist, was not put off as were the liberals of an earlier generation, such as Adolf Harnack, by Barth's language about God as the "unknown" and above all as the "wholly other"—an appellation that Barth was to regret, but one that Bultmann never abandoned. Barth had not apparently foreseen that, despite his anti-liberal tirades, a God who was "wholly other" would become meat and drink to liberal theologians committed to the principle that while God may clearly be a reality, what we can say about God must always take the form of a statement concerning our transformed existences.

5

Postliberal Theology and the Camel's Nose

A PERSISTENT UNDERCURRENT in much of the argumentation of the last several chapters is the contention that human beings do not and cannot live without convictions concerning the truth of things. Not just spiritually but even pragmatically, personal and communal existence is simply inconceivable without deeply held assumptions that can be variously stamped religious, metaphysical, ontological—the lines between them being sometimes fuzzy—from which the human enterprise takes its inspiration.

Fairly early on in the Christian West, Augustine drew his rather dark conclusion about humanity from the fact that human beings need to believe; to wit, human beings are created to worship, and thus if they do not know the *true* God, they will create an idol and worship the creature instead of the creator. Earlier Paul had held a similar doctrine, but the apparent darkness of Paul's ruminations about human history, nature, and destiny in the early chapters of Romans finds its culmination in the brilliant light of his declaration: "For God has consigned all men to disobedience, that he may have mercy upon all."[1] Augustine, on the other hand, read humanity's penchant for idolatry in harsh consistency with his terrible doctrine of predestination. Either our lives and convictions are shaped by God's electing grace or it turns out that even our virtues must finally be seen as a species of our idolatry. They are,

1. Rom 11:32.

at best, as Augustine has been held to have said, "splendid vices"—good things done for the wrong, that is, godless, reasons.[2]

Augustine is not presently *en vogue*. Even such a secularized version of Augustinian themes as Marxism has crumbled from within. Nevertheless, the tendency to see the problem of religious epistemology in the light of the dialectic between salvation and damnation is still being dragged to the door of traditional Western Christianity.

It is the glory of theological liberalism that it has led to a widespread rejection of the traditional claim that orthodox belief is a prerequisite to salvation. Yet liberalism, in reacting against the notion that one is saved by orthodox belief, did so in such a manner as to open the door to shallow doctrinal relativism. Thus it has become something of a modern cliché to dismiss the problem of the diversity of human beliefs by relativizing all belief until one belief is as good as any other. Thus the vulgarism: "Everyone has a right to his or her own opinion." This pop relativism is preferable to the more sophisticated nihilism of the intelligentsia—a nihilism oddly enough assumed by such diverse ideologies as scientism and existentialism. Nihilism shares with these latter the idea that the convictional foundations of human existence are illusions. Thus, ironically, it becomes for nihilism a matter of the highest conviction that all foundational belief must be rooted out and destroyed.

The reticence of more traditional theology to speak in clear and definite words about its faith has developed partly from its proper reluctance to counter relativism and nihilism with the brutal predestinarian logic of the Augustinian tradition (or its Pelagian counterpart) that unbelievers deserve to be damned because right belief is one of the works necessary unto salvation. Most Christians cannot bring themselves to regard all modern culture as merely a splendid vice; moreover, they intuitively recognize that the love they have known in Jesus Christ precludes the various logics of dam-

2. Augustine never used the phrase "splendid vices" (*vitia splendida*), although the essential idea is arguably found in the *City of God* XIX.25. See Wetzel, "Splendid Vices and Secular Virtues," 271.

nation employed by earlier Christians to defend theological truth. Therefore, it is vainly imagined that if we keep our beliefs soft and vague—but at the same time rhetorically edifying—then we need not face the logical implication that if some theological utterances are true, then opposite opinions must be false—indeed, heretical.

Not all Christians, of course, have troubled consciences in these matters. Many have been able to make a virtue of necessity and simply celebrate the currently popular metaphysical and religious pluralism and relativism. For some, it is simply unambiguously wonderful that religious and/or metaphysical convictions abound. Christianity, Judaism, Islam, Hinduism, Buddhism, idealism, materialism, pragmatism, skepticism, and so on, are merely "local truths" or individual expressions of a universal human need. None need be thought truer or more erroneous than any other; in fact, to argue so would to be non-inclusive, imperialistic, and discriminatory.

Yet it is difficult to see how such relativism could be merged with the substance of the Christian faith, for it must be asked how such a relativism differs from a *de facto* denial of the God of Jesus Christ. Sensing this, many Christians adopt pluralistic relativism with a vague uneasiness of conscience. Most Christians cannot embrace such radical extremes as the current nihilisms that deny all spiritual and ethical truth. How can a Christian look to Jesus Christ and deny that there is truth? He *is* the truth. Yet, on the other hand, how does one affirm this truth with emphasis and vigor and not be deemed a bigoted Christian chauvinist? Christians are by no means universally enthusiastic about relativism, indeterminacy, and theological evasiveness, but the nerve to forthright theological affirmation has been severed.

How tempting it is, then, to try to avoid the charge of being anachronistic or dogmatic by doing theologies that allow one, when the going gets rough, to make soft ontological claims. It has been argued and, I hope, demonstrated that soft theological ontologies result either in a denial of God's genuine self-giving in Jesus Christ, or, as exemplified by such giants as Bultmann and Tillich—who affirm (however paradoxically) God's self-giving—unstable systems of theological equivocation.

Further, it has been argued that not only Christology but even Christian ethics is destabilized by a consistent *via negativa*. An examination of Kaufman and McFague has shown that their ethical intention is radically subverted by their penchant for theological equivocation. If no hard reasons, reasons grounded in the truth of things, stand behind their ethical advice, such advice is easily reduced to little more than emotive self-indulgence.

Finally, it has been argued that all such undertakings to do theology in terms of a soft ontology (seemingly required in such species as metaphorical theology, symbolic theology, and the like) upon scrutiny reveal underlying hard ontological assumptions that expose the pretense of a genuine, consistent, non-dogmatic theological equivocation. I hope it has been made clear that it is crucial to the integrity of the whole theological enterprise that theologians admit that they do, in fact, in the term of the deconstructionists, "privilege" their assumptions of a real and actual "presence" or truth or reality on which they base their theological utterances. Rather than being somehow embarrassed, Christian theology should glory in such privileging, for its object is God. But beyond the honor afforded in being privileged to privilege God, the privileging of one's basic assumptions is a function of the condition of human existence. Everyone, including those in the deconstructionist movement itself, privileges his or her own enterprise. It is already too late to beat the deconstructionists to the punch. They have already begun to expose our secret atheisms; nevertheless, it is never too late for Christians to admit that they believe in something real.

The spectacle of Christians witnessing to Jesus Christ and claiming to privilege no truth or belief, remaining ever so ontologically coy by either moralizing doctrine (the more traditionalist approach) or metaphorizing it (*à la* the neo-liberal revisionists), and then to have dragged from them against their wills that they as Christians do, in fact, believe something after all, is humiliating beyond words.

Our present theological mood bears certain parallels—if somewhat upside-down parallels—to the early years of the Trinitarian controversy. When the controversy first erupted the majority in the Eastern Church would have preferred to remain vaguely in the middle of the struggle unfolding between the Trinitarian party of Alexander and Athanasius, and the Arians. For many Christians, the Trinitarian doctrine that the Son was eternally the Son of the Father seemed to violate the best philosophic wisdom of their time as well as Old Testament monotheism. Plato's and Aristotle's understanding of the transcendence of God, for example, forbade God's direct involvement in the world; likewise, in their view, God's oneness precluded God's communicating his essence. Yet it was the vital faith of those same Christians that in the life and work of Jesus Christ they had been saved. Further, the liturgy of the church made unabashed Arianism religiously obnoxious. Arianism would have it that "Son of God" was a mere courtesy title, for in the last analysis the Son was a demigod and thus a creature.

Caught in conflicting commitments between a static monotheism and the saving power of Jesus Christ, the majority resented the controversy, for they were simply not prepared or capacitated to embark upon the laborious process of recasting their monotheism. Finally, however, the pressure of the options forced upon it by the debate between the Athanasians and the Arians drove the church, albeit reluctantly, to take a clear stand. It was a stand that, however intertwined it might have been with the philosophic biases of its day, however philosophic its actual language (*homoousia*, consubstantial, etc.) might be, nevertheless finally sided with the revelation of God in Jesus Christ over a philosophic or unitarian reading of Old Testament monotheism. Perhaps, as liberalism has concluded, this was a disastrous error, and the ancient bishops should have sided with Arius. Nevertheless, the effect of the Trinitarian controversy was to drive unconscious or conscious vagueness to the ground. George A. Lindbeck has noted the ramifications of controversy in more general terms: "Controversy is the normal means whereby implicit doctrines become explicit, and operational ones official."[3] Oh, that this were indeed the universal norm! The protracted fight between Trinitarians and anti-Trinitarians, traditionalists and liberals, in the modern era has not produced explicit and official doctrine. It has produced internal hemorrhaging and theological obfuscation. The modern ecumenical movement, despite its progress in enlarging understanding *between* denominations, has not in the least been able to heal the Trinitarian/anti-Trinitarian split *within* denominations, which makes the other debates between denominations seem trivial by comparison.

At one level, one might think our present cultural climate potentially more open to the doctrine of the Trinity than was the fourth century, for fourth-century Hellenistic philosophy was not receptive to the notion that God could suffer. The cross of the Son of God was an enormous stumbling block to a claim that he was genuinely "of God." In our age, however, insofar as there is much faith in God left among the "cultured," it is not in a God conceived in terms of radical impassibility. Would this not appear to commend Trinitarian faith? If God is a suffering God and if he is claimed to have been made manifest in the person of his Son, would it not be expected that the Son should suffer? Would not suffering be at least a partial verification of the presence in Jesus Christ of such a God?

Of course, such a surmise would be naïve. For just as the ancient philosophic doctrine of divine impassibility (which held sway as late as the Deist period) conceived of God as radically transcendent and thereby excluded even the possibility of his suffering involvement in the world, so our present understanding of God's passibility, though it is a radically immanent passibility, now renders talk of God's transcendence inconceivable.

Clearly the most prominent, though not the first philosophic, exponent of divine suffering has been Alfred North Whitehead.[4]

---

3. Lindbeck, *Nature of Doctrine*, 75.

4. See my reply to John Cobb's claim of Whiteheadian originality, "Process Theology Debate Continues," 224–25.

In Whitehead's bipolar theism God in his suffering, consequent nature is indivisible from the evolutionary process of the cosmos itself. The idea of immanental divine suffering has been influential well beyond Whitehead's school of process theology, as McFague and Kaufman illustrate. Clearly, there is simply no place in such naturalism for Trinitarianism, at least Trinitarianism that is even remotely related to the Trinitarianism of the fourth century, for the latter is inconceivable apart from the unique initiative of the transcendent God, an initiative that immanental naturalism must regard as a priori unthinkable.

Indeed, Sallie McFague styles her own immanentalism as deliberately subversive of Trinitarianism. Her threefold conception of God as "mother, lover, and friend" is, she acknowledges, not coincidental, but a "deliberate attempt to unseat" the names Father, Son, and Holy Spirit. Yet this is "no subterfuge to establish a new trinity [sic] using different names. To do so would be to fall into the 'tyranny of absolutizing imagination'" which, she insists, she has diligently avoided. No, her proposal is more "modest." McFague merely wants to show that models other than those of traditional Christian theology can be "appropriate" and "illuminating." Given this, one might expect some modest gesture in the direction of what these proposed alternative models—models independent of those of traditional Christian theology—might look like. One, however, would look in vain, for McFague offers no original models. What she proposes instead is the expropriation of traditional Christian theological categories and their assimilation to her "new holistic sensibility." Nothing is to escape this ransacking: God as creator, savior, and sustainer, as well as the classical loci of creation, salvation, revelation, sin, evil—each is to be colonized and "reoriented" to her "understanding of the gospel as destabilizing, inclusive, non-hierarchical fulfillment." Perhaps, she airily muses, these classical motifs will offer "a habitable house in which to live for a while, with doors open and windows ajar, and with the promise that additions and renovations are desired and needed."[5]

5. McFague, *Models of God*, 181–82.

One might be forgiven if one finds lurking in such fustian rhetoric the very tyranny that McFague would purportedly eschew. Clearly, McFague sees the logical impossibility of tying her immanental theism to Trinitarianism, but she is not quite able, given her residual Christianity, to quite let go altogether. In this she constitutes but one expression of the general ambivalence of a whole era of academic American theologians, but even more significantly, of theologians teaching in the mainline seminaries, men and women who are immanental unitarians to the core, but who in the context of the church continue to couch their will to theological and socio-political power almost entirely in terms of the language of the Triune God whom they have repudiated and abandoned.

I cannot believe that the whole American theological community is made up of either atheists or unitarians, covert or overt. God has kept to himself at least seven thousand who have not bowed the knee to Baal. The quiescence of the theological community in the face of the theological erosion of so seemingly vital a doctrine as the Trinity—the ever vigilant Robert W. Jenson being one notable exception[6]—which entails the question of the very divinity of Christ, is not attributable to the fact that no one believes in that divinity anymore, for many still do. It is my suspicion that the reason much of the reluctance of more traditional theologians to call the turn on such systematic unbelief or half-belief is that traditional theology has its own dirty little secret to keep.

Clearly neo-liberalism has savaged the tradition in the name of the modern philosophical concept of God as suffering immanence. Yet, without embracing the doctrine of a God ontologically limited in power so endemic to neo-liberalism, traditional theology has itself, in its own way, presumably for more "biblical" reasons, undergone a revolution that has shifted the axis of its doctrine of God away from a concept of transcendence that sees divinity in terms of triumphalist, predestining, impassible power to one

---

6. See Jenson, *God According to the Gospel*, and, more recently, the first volume of his *Systematic Theology*.

that equates divinity with suffering. Many traditional Christians speak of God's lordship in the world as supremely manifested in the *kenosis* and suffering of Jesus Christ, the Son of God. Yet there has not been a general facing up to the theological implications required by such a shift. Having made very little attempt to integrate this momentous shift of its doctrine of God into every other aspect of doctrine, traditional theology has little sense as to where its *ad hoc* theopaschitism might lead. I think that there is an abiding, repressed fear on the part of traditional theologians that perhaps such a drastic transformation of its doctrine of God's impassibility may prove simply too destructive of the rest of the tradition, and that it is thus best to carry on the pretense that they can alter a monumental theological premise and then go on with business as usual on all other fronts. Could it be that traditional theologians, were they to try to come to terms with their own theopaschitism, would be driven into a variety of liberal reductionisms against their wills? What if the atheism that traditional theology quietly or publicly suspects to be lurking in the heart of the liberal can secretly be found in its own heart as well?

Tactically the neo-liberal, anti-Trinitarian exponents of theological indeterminacy have been brilliant. They have used the alleged indeterminacy of their theological language as a smoke screen behind which to attack the Christian tradition and to hide aspects of their own naturalistic intentions while at the same time styling themselves as making modest theological assertions. For their part, traditional theologians have used such givens as the imperfection of human speech and understanding as a means by which to beat their retreat or to justify theological inertia—as an excuse for not coming to theological terms with the theological revolution they have inherited.

My own reflections here being in no sense an exception, if traditional theology contents itself with proving, at least to its own satisfaction, that it can map out the philosophical minefields and show that there is a path through for theological speech after all, then all that its labors will have produced is what is already self-evident. It will have accomplished nothing more than the theological counterpart of the reinvention of the wheel. It is almost embarrassing to find theologians breathing a sigh of relief because they can demonstrate that God-talk is possible. Of course it is possible! Go to almost any church and you will hear it.

Writing soon after World War II and thus on the threshold of the great neo-liberal rush to indeterminacy, the neo-Thomistic theologian E. L Mascall observed that theology does not probe into the nature of theological speech in order to determine whether or not such speech is possible. Rather, theology undertakes its linguistic analysis in order "to account for the fact that discourse about God has, as a matter of experience, been taking place in spite of various considerations that might seem at first sight to rule its possibility out of court."[7]

Despite the slogging frustrations of the journey, I cannot summon even a foggy notion as to how it would be possible to avoid trekking through the ever-shifting modern epistemological morass. Many actually suppose they are on the verge of charting it. Forty-one years ago, Mascall made an observation concerning the epistemological climate at that time, and while the philosophic style and cast of characters have drastically changed, the overall prejudice of our moment bears a distressing similarity to the situation Mascall then described.

> The recurrent tendency among philosophers in analysing the mental activities of human beings in general, [is] to assume that until their analysis and criticism have been satisfactorily completed, nobody has the right to make any affirmations at all; so deeply has Cartesianism entered into our heritage. The consequence is that the plain man laughs at the philosophers and goes on his own way without them.[8]

The "plain man" may indeed laugh, but the theologian cannot. Even if one takes the revelationist advice of Kierkegaard to the

---

7. Mascall, *Existence and Analogy*, 95.
8. Ibid., 94.

effect that since revealed truth appears absurd to natural reason, finally the only way to deal with modern skepticism is to break with it and stand utterly on revelation, still one would have to take note of skepticism in order to break with it (as Kierkegaard himself did so brilliantly). Thus, ironically, to the extent that even non-apologetic theologians enter the epistemological fray, they not only create more fodder for skepticism to feed upon, but by entertaining the barbs of the skeptics, allow them to get under their skin. Mascall, who was critical of what he took to be the philosophic shortsightedness of the "revelationist," nevertheless, as a Thomist himself, gave first place to revealed truth. Finally, not without irony, Mascall, an Aristotelian rationalist Christian, in his own way accepted the advice of Kierkegaard the existentialist Christian and broke with modern Cartesianism not only in the name of Thomas and Aristotle but above all in the name of Jesus Christ. Yet in so doing he, too, had to come to terms with the modern skeptical tradition that was the very orbit from which he ultimately wanted to escape.

William Placher, whom many regard as a postliberal theologian (a position that might be understood as moderate Barthianism), is sensitive to the ironies implicit in a traditional theologian attempting to be thoroughly informed by contemporary epistemology while remaining only provisionally open to it. Given the title of his significant book, *Unapologetic Theology*, one might expect Placher to reject even a provisional openness to philosophy but instead to don Tertullian's anti-apologetic mantle, declaring philosophy irrelevant to theology. Placher recognizes a certain paradox in his undertaking. While insisting that "Christians ought to speak in their own voice and not worry about finding philosophical 'foundations' for their claims," he nevertheless acknowledges that he draws extensively from the work of philosophers in order to establish epistemologically that such independence is possible.[9] The question is, can a purportedly independent and self-justifying

---

9. Placher, *Unapologetic Theology*, 13.

theology team itself with an equally independent, wildly pluralistic philosophic environment and manage a synthesis that will achieve its theological goals?

After Placher offers a very impressive and helpful survey of a great number of philosophic perspectives, he tends to ride off in two directions at the same time. The one direction entails a somewhat defensive, "unapologetic" apologetic use of cultural pluralism, while the other direction is more genuinely unapologetic. In the last analysis, it illustrates the failure, albeit the high-level failure, that must attend any attempt to undergird a Barthian revelationism with philosophy or cultural analysis. The fact that Placher cannot achieve a fully coherent synthesis between his philosophic preferences and his Barthian Christianity is nonetheless instructive and provides evidence that only a more radical Barthianism is of any avail if one is to resist the temptation to let one's philosophic predilections or one's reading of the current *Weltgeist* to have the first and, of necessity, the last word.

On his defensive tack, Placher reviews a number of those thinkers he styles as still embracing the Enlightenment's rationalistic dream that there exists some universal standard of rationality. Placher is not quite certain whether the Enlightenment is dead or whether its imperialistic claim that it has the key to all truth remains the chief obstacle to traditional Christianity's getting a respectful hearing. But living or dead, Enlightenment rationalism is the chief villain of Placher's piece. I must confess here that I find Enlightenment rationality in all its imperiousness a good deal healthier then some of the varieties of relativism, nihilism, and skepticism that Placher drags in to undo the intellectual imperialism of rationalism. For example, I would take a state governed by the light of a Thomas Jefferson's belief in a universal standard of rationality over the anarchism of Michel Foucault. From Descartes through the Enlightenment, to neo-Marxists and closet positivists, the presupposition that there is but one, true, objective, sane, rational way to grasp the truth is a unifying motif in philosophies that are otherwise disparate. Against such intellectual exclusivism,

Placher marshals a very broad, pluralistic range of relativistic critiques—from the cultural relativism of anthropologists, to the dark, self-destructive nihilism of Michel Foucault, to the preppy nihilism of Richard Rorty, to the calculated but seemingly bemused relativism of Wittgenstein's language games, to the perennial disagreements among philosophers of science about how science—the most positive of all human undertakings—actually functions. In all this, Placher attempts to show that the Enlightenment dream of a monolithic rationality is a chimera.

But does not such radical pluralism make an unstable foundation on which to present the Christian faith? Can one build on the argument that since many philosophers are no longer persuaded by the Enlightenment ideal of a monolithic rationality, theology need not be cowed into silence since the Enlightenment no longer carries the authority to silence the din even within its own philosophical house? Perhaps the most obvious question is, once Placher has used the pluralistic climate to attack Enlightenment rationalism, how is he going to get the relativism, nihilism, and skepticism that feeds such pluralism off his back? It is immediately clear that Placher himself does not believe that the world is random and meaningless; on the contrary, in his view, it is the creation of God and all will finally see its higher unity.

One line Placher employs in order to keep from slipping into the camp of a doctrinaire pluralism is to show that even such seeming relativists as Foucault or Rorty, though they claim there is no truth, operate clearly out of less than open fundamental assumptions. Indeed, they are truly genuinely relativistic only at those points not directly germane to their own beliefs. Thus, they not only assume the superiority of their own views, but on the basis of that assumption are intolerant of others.

At this point I do not think that Placher is fully cognizant of the implications of his own data. The problem is not just one of the Enlightenment rearing its intolerant head. As has been argued throughout these pages, neither relativism, nor skepticism, nor nihilism—indeed no conceivable position—can immunize itself from the fact that everyone must believe something in order even to start to think. Therefore, every position, even the most tolerant and well-meaning, when placed in tension with other positions, can be forced to expose its non-negotiable, overarching assumptions about the nature and limits of rationality. Other perspectives are no less absolute than the Enlightenment perspective when they are pushed. The fact is that we powerfully believe whatever it is that we do come to believe. Thus, one must ask: can the very pluralism that arises out of violently conflicting modern beliefs legitimately be seen as the way to an epistemological version of the peaceable kingdom?

Clearly, the historical roots of pluralism lie not in the conscious abandonment of the Enlightenment ideal and a deliberate march toward universal pluralism. Modern and postmodern pluralism came into being by default. They arose out of the proliferation of mutually exclusive metaphysics, anti-metaphysics, ideologies, anti-ideologies, etc., none of which have been able to command the assent of a wide audience, although any among them would be happy to claim ascendancy if such ascendancy were attainable. The pluralistic mindset has emerged from the chaos of the modern breakdown of shared convictions. Such pluralism that is the product of the ceaseless competition of ideas cannot be tamed, harnessed, or turned from its assignation with relativism, skepticism and nihilism and become a species of what Placher calls "tolerant pluralism."[10] If it could, pluralism would no longer be the random, ever-growing, unpredictable, fragmentizing phenomenon it has become. It would instead be a phenomenon potentially controllable—controllable by the virtue of tolerance.

Indeed, where have we seen such tolerance? Placher certainly cannot claim to see it in the academy. The academy constitutes a potpourri of tunnel-visioned specialists and Enlightenment, liberal, Marxist, Freudian, behaviorist, and feminist ideologues. Placher himself is concerned that Christianity not be consumed

10. Ibid., 106.

by the relativizing tendencies of the academy. He salutes the "determination" of postliberal theologians "to preserve a distinctively Christian voice."[11] Could it be that the desire for tolerant pluralism is more a mythic ideal than a description of how actual pluralism really works? That there are limits to the tolerance people of any tradition can or will allow themselves? There are, to be sure, family resemblances between traditions, ideologies, or perceived mutual interests that make certain conversations between mutually exclusive traditions useful. However, those traditions that cannot be made to fit are ignored or despised. If we are honest, we have neither the time nor, more importantly, the inclination to talk in depth to everyone. The best we can hope for is an uneven, limited tolerance. Indeed, we must honestly acknowledge that pluralism closes as many conversations as it opens.

Clearly, Placher's vision of a "tolerant pluralism," and the value he places on inclusive conversation between people of radically divergent views, flows directly from Placher's own ultimate convictions. He believes, for example, that all humanity is created in God's image, which is the primal reason for openness; that human knowledge is inevitably incomplete but virtually none of it is wholly irredeemably so; that all knowledge is rooted in the particularities and temporalities of tradition, but conversation between individuals standing firm in their own tradition can nonetheless be mutually fruitful in strengthening the commitment of each conversationalist to his or her own tradition.

Placher, like Jeffrey Stout,[12] is much impressed by anthropologist Claude Levi-Strauss' model of the *bricoleur*, the tinkerer, the jack-of-all-trades who squirrels away odd tools, fragments of materials, and bits of string in readiness for some as yet unknown future use. The methodology of the *bricoleur* with its *ad hoc* rationality and catch-as-catch-can pragmatism, modestly taking help from wherever it is found, makes itself at home not only in its own

---

11. Ibid., 169.
12. Stout, *Ethics After Babel*, 74–75; Placher, *Unapologetic Theology*, 67.

more primitive environment but also in the "authentic pluralism" that Placher believes characterizes the best the world can offer.

Placher believes that Christianity has something that is universally true to say, yet he recognizes that apart from faith people are not able to embrace that truth; thus the paradox that universal truth is not universally known. *Bricolage* is an epistemological methodology ideally suited to those in whose worldview human knowledge is conceived of as incurably paradoxical or metaphorical or fragmented or flawed or radically limited by finitude or even sin—any or all of the above. It is an attempt to make the best of the indeterminacy and pluralism that is humanity's plight if not its glory.

Yet it must be asked, what of those who see radical intellectual pluralism as a function of the yet imperfect progress of human knowledge? What of someone like the cosmologist Stephen W. Hawking, who in his quest for a "theory of everything" has not despaired of what Placher characterizes as the Enlightenment ideal of a single standard of rationality?[13] Hawking perhaps has the sheer genius and undaunted pluck to carry such a thing off. Merely because the Newtonian universe was overturned after two hundred years of regnancy does not mean that we may not see again such a synthesizing construct.

One can well imagine that to such persons, *bricolage*—open conversation come one and come all—might appear to be nothing but a time-wasting excursion back into the Dark Ages, or dilettantism, or a diverting vacation from serious work but largely irrelevant to the *real* quest. To be sure, the *real* quest is limited to an extremely elite number of mathematical and scientific geniuses. But if it succeeds it would relegate the *bricoleur*, with all due regard for his primitive resourcefulness, back to the pre-scientific past whence he came. Could it be that appeals to the *bricoleur* are a symptom of a cultural loss of nerve at the very time when the new Newton may be at the gates?

---

13. Hawking, *Short History of Time*.

My own intuition tells me that the universe will forever throw up to us mysteries, so that not even the greatest of geniuses now or in the future will ever be able to toss a conceptual blanket around it and solve every riddle. I can, nevertheless, respect those who don't think so and are prepared to follow Hawking on the quest for a theory of everything. But curiously, I suspect so would Placher as well. He is too genuinely tolerant and open to an *a priori* pronouncement against the very quest for so potentially a monolithic vision of reality and knowledge. Still, he does smart at the intolerance of those who have no use for his own tradition (Reformed Christianity). Placher is critical of such philosophers as John Rawls and Richard Rorty who simply have no time for those views they discern as radically out of phase with their own liberal rationalism or relativism. Placher charges them with "dismissing as 'insane' those who do not share enough of our own cultural assumptions—the very opposite of tolerant pluralism."[14] Thus, in effect, he breaks with them. Alas, there are always limits even to the most tolerant of pluralisms.

For my part, I think that Placher is correct in claiming that it is in the very nature of Christianity to require that Christians seek conversation, not just with the non-religious but with believers of other faiths, even when the terms of the conversation require a sincere commitment to bracket attempts to convert on both sides of the exchange. There are all sorts of theological reasons for this—the doctrine of creation, the love of Christ, but also fleshy reasons as well: the pleasure of simple human mutuality, even simple human curiosity, commend conversation. Placher points out that such an exchange can be pragmatically useful if only in helping to deepen our insights into our own traditions, for in dialogue our beliefs are passed through the prism of the other, and at its best such dialogue produces a mutually deepening experience for all partners involved. Thus, for example, the Christian becomes a better Christian as the Buddhist becomes a better Buddhist. But for Christians even

---

14. Placher, *Unapologetic Theology*, 106.

such minimal utilitarianism need not be evoked in order to justify conversation. For Christians and for many other people, simple, warm, respectful, human intercourse is of value for its own sake. However, do I have the right, to say nothing of the stomach, to engage in mutually open conversation with a Nazi, particularly a Nazi in power? How would this differ from collaboration? If I were to converse with a Nazi, it would be in order to find ways to thwart him. Or what of a devil cultist on his way home from a human sacrifice? Or a decent, kind Christian Scientist, a good neighbor, a lover of ecological causes, a nuclear pacifist, but one who wants to withhold medical treatment from his desperately ill child? Can I legitimize engaging in open-ended, non-conversional theological conversation with him or her, or is it better perhaps that I kidnap the child and bring her to the hospital? Or what about my neighborhood astrologer? How much time must I waste wrangling with her, when I believe heart and soul that the stars lead us nowhere? And so it goes. Not everyone, in good conscience or in good spirit, can deeply converse with everyone else. This is one of the fragmenting symptoms of modern pluralism.

Placher is an intelligent, tolerant, fair, open-minded Christian scholar, and as such he takes certain umbrage at being lumped with the insane. Nevertheless, there are many people, particularly among the intelligentsia, who, seeing no final difference between the religion of Jim Jones and that of John Calvin, do not have much use for any of us Christians. And I can see their point. If there were no God, we are all most certainly cranks.

One of the great problems with apologetic defenses of Christianity, even Placher's unapologetic form, is the obvious "risk" they run of "cutting and trimming the gospel to fit it to the categories and assumptions of a particular philosophical or cultural position."[15] However, beyond this are the inevitable negative consequences of tying the Christian proclamation to a particular reading of the cultural moment or to one or another of the philosophic positions that have come or will come down the philosophic pike, be

---

15. Ibid., 160.

it Platonism, Aristotelianism, Hegelianism, Nietzschean, existentialism, deconstructionism, or whatever awaits on the philosophic horizon. Ironically, despite the intention of apologetic theology to make Christianity more generally available, often the opposite effect results. Each particular apologetic serves to *limit* the general appeal of Christianity by wedding it to a position that in the nature of the mutual exclusiveness of the great philosophic options must exclude all the other positions. The Christian gospel's capacity to cut through all cultural and ideological differences is not served. The cumulative effect of apologetic following apologetic is a parochializing of the faith, the attempt to band it to one or another of the fashions of a particular historical moment. Even Tillich, whose method of correlation in theory was supposed to render him radically open to the world in all its diversity, was himself so much the product of German idealism and existentialism that he had no use for what he disdainfully called "supranaturalism," presumably the Platonic and Aristotelian traditions, and he was downright hostile to the Anglo-American positivist tradition. Thus, Tillich's existentialist apologetic is potentially a barrier to more people in America than it is an aid. America has never so despaired of its Enlightenment, rationalist heritage as to become widely enamored of existentialism as have many German and French intellectuals. The limiting impact of apologetics on the gospel's universal appeal is almost comically the case with process theology and its dependence on Whitehead. The claim of Whiteheadian process theologians is that Whitehead provides the means by which Christianity can be made relevant to the modern world. However, hardly anyone in the intellectual world reads Whitehead these days. Rather than a means by which Christianity is made more universally available, Whitehead becomes yet another hurdle that believers must leap in order to make their Whiteheadian way to faith. Before one can be led to accept Christianity, it would seem that one first must read, digest, and believe in Whitehead. But how, one wonders, is a believer who is an astrophysicist to deal, for example, with the fact that for reasons critical to his philosophy, Whitehead thought

Einstein was wrong on the question of gravity and he, Whitehead, was right?[16]

Placher would seem to avoid these dual perils of apologetic theology—reductionism and parochialism—because his use of philosophy is eclectic and *ad hoc*. Indeed, many philosophers he cites are either used as foils or as handmaidens to his theological purposes. He is in the first place not a philosopher. He is above all a believing Christian. But does this not create an "unapologetic" backlash of its own? Theologians can have no personal grounds on which to complain when Placher uses philosophers as pawns on his theological chess board. Most do likewise. Yet is this not to be reading each philosophy at arms length, i.e., as a Christian with no expectation or intention that the philosophic perspective will become one's own? And thus, is not the value of philosophy relativized by the place one makes for it in what is to philosophy an alien undertaking, i.e., Christian theology? As a Christian theologian, I cannot help but feel my faith relativized when I see it analyzed from the perspective of any non-Christian philosophy or religion. There is no way out of this.

I can see how philosophers themselves, in seeing their work used to an end that places it in an alien theological perspective, might feel they were not so much engaged in conversation as exploited. How many philosophers reading Placher's book would conclude that he is writing in the spirit of tolerant pluralism and how many would conclude quite the opposite: that Placher and his interlocutors stand so fixed in their traditions or convictional orbits that while "conversation" is carried out, it is carried out only under a flag of truce from within what might be described as intellectually armed camps? Indeed, they would conclude that Placher is engaged in "conversation" in order to establish definitively the limits of all conversation.

Despite his *ad hoc*, eclectic use of philosophy, despite his refusal to commit to any single philosophy—so that he cannot be pigeonholed as an apologist along Whiteheadian, or Wittgensteinian,

---

16. Whitehead, *Principle of Relativity*.

or Heideggerian, or neo-Thomist lines—I fear that having given philosophy the *first* word in his understanding of pluralism and relativism, Placher cannot with consistency deny it the last word as well. Of course, consistency be damned, he calls halt on the claims of philosophy before he comes under its control, but he does so by what many might seem an arbitrary break. After he has full use of philosophy, he returns to his genuinely unapologetic stance and speaks as a man of faith. Why not dispense with the red herrings and speak as a theologian from the beginning? Surely the theologian can discuss the tensions between monolithic rational schemes and pluralistic visions on theological grounds. Perhaps such an approach might genuinely shed new light on the matter. Could it be that in the sovereignty and omniscience of God we can find grounds to appreciate the desire for a universal standard of rationality? Perhaps in God's creation of free men and women, we can find a way to place an otherwise avaricious pluralism in theological perspective.

However, Placher has in the last analysis placed himself in a no-man's-land between the many various philosophic readings of modern pluralism on the one hand and what I take to be one of the critical genuine theological tasks before us in a pluralistic age—a genuine theology of pluralism. What is desperately needed is a biblically grounded, theologically conversant assessment of pluralism in which Christians can "speak in their own voice and not worry about finding philosophical 'foundations' for their claims."[17] Placher does not offer such, for he would have to break with his defensive apologetic stance to achieve such theological independence. Rather than parroting back to a pluralistic world its pluralistic reading of its own pluralism, theology should speak on the assumption that the key to understanding human diversity lies in God's disclosure of who he is and what he is doing in a world so plural.

For its part, the world's response to the phenomenon of its own pluralism has included a perfect catalogue of horrors—from

17. Placher, *Unapologetic Theology*, 13.

political totalitarianism, to nihilism, to skepticism and cynicism, to the easy careless relativisms that are rampant about us. Do Christians have to be reminded that none of the various words spoken by the world about itself are the same as the Word that became flesh? Christian openness and the tolerance born of Christ's love cannot be constructed out of a world-weary despair for the truth. To construct a Christian theological assessment out of even the best wisdom of a world torn apart by its own diversity not only relegates God's self-disclosure to second place, but from the point of view of the world, it offers nothing that the world does not already know.

To Christianity's shame, what is included in what the world already knows is the forlorn history in which too much of the Christian tradition has provided its terrible "answer" to the question of pluralism. Indeed, there are many Christian horrors to be faced up to. Throughout its history, on grounds of honoring the truth it had discovered in Christ, the church met its own as well as the world's pluralism with persecution, censorship, and general disapprobation. It is at this point, if theology is to deal persuasively with modern pluralism, that it must begin by coming to terms with what the world already knows and acknowledge the manifest sins against human diversity in its own tradition. Without this, anything Christian theology says to the pluralistic situation will be a transparent cover-up or a cliché.

The Bible is the only place to start a genuine theology of pluralism. It ranges far and wide on the question of the tensions that exist between diversity and faithfulness, including faithful speech about God: from Elijah's slaughter of the 450 priests of Baal, to Paul's claim that "God has consigned all men to disobedience that he might have mercy upon all"; from the Johannine witness that "God is love," to Jesus' apocalyptic pronouncements about hell; from the story of the tower of Babel in which God is portrayed as threatened by human ingenuity as well as our understandable concerns for flood control, to the first story of creation in which human ingenuity and creative initiative (that inevitably produces pluralistic diversity) is not just permitted, but commanded: "Be fruitful and multiply, and fill the earth and subdue it."[18]

What is needed is a theological undertaking to weave these and a hundred other passages into a theological celebration of the role of the suffering God in the rich diversity of human culture, but which does not blanch from or ignore the fact that not all we do is approved and tolerated by God. The God in whose creative will we ourselves are called to be creative is also the jealous God of judgment and wrath. The God who loves us in our diversity is also the God who suffers when our diversity becomes an expression of our self-destructive rebellion. The God who in righteous fury struck out at the fragmenting of the human race through its rebellion and who hit his beloved Son who was standing in our stead is not a God of uncomplicated tolerance. In short, Christian theology must find its own voice in addressing those questions of supreme import to a pluralistic world that the world cannot raise for itself. Only a theology that declares its independence from the start is able to raise questions the answers to which will not be a mere rehash of the world's wisdom.

Theological speech about pluralism ought rightly to begin not in an epistemological investigation of the possibility of speech in a pluralistic environment, but in matters of radically theological concern: What was God doing in creation? In what ways are we called to be co-creators? What is the difference between creativity and rebellion? How can we explore the line between pluralism and license, which is a manifestation of our sin? Certainly we cannot be so gullible as to imagine that the world's understanding of its own pluralism can substitute for a Christian theological understanding. The world advances all sorts of half-truths and in some cases downright lies in seeking to understand its diversity. An understanding of pluralism that opens the door to utter relativism, to skepticism, or to nihilism is false on the face of it. To imagine that God's variety requires one or another species of despair for

---

18. 1 Kgs 18:21–40; Rom 11:32; 1 John 4:8; Matt 5:22, 29–30; 10:28; 23:15, 33; Mark 9:43–48; Luke 12:5; Gen 1:26–28.

the very possibility of truth is to misunderstand not just truth, but pluralistic variety as well.

If theology took such a tack on pluralism, that is, if theologians talked liked theologians, the question of the possibility of God-talk in a pluralistic age would take care of itself. For we would be proving the possibility of God-talk in the only way in which that possibility can be established—by doing it. The task of theological epistemology would not be dependent on theologians finding a philosophic way out of the Cartesian impasse. The task of theological epistemology would be similar to the work of the grammarian. Grammarians don't argue whether language is possible. They observe how language is used and seek to systematize its use by the ex post facto inferring of rules for grammatical speech.

When Placher switches gears from his unapologetic-apologetic theology to that of a genuinely unapologetic theologian, he is aware of all of this, as well as aware of the dangers of this grammatical analogy if it is pushed beyond theological epistemology to the whole of Christian doctrine. Thus, he warns postliberal theologians (such Yalies as George Lindbeck, David Kelsey, and the late Hans Frei) that they risk sounding like radical relativists in claiming, along the lines of Lindbeck, "that Christian doctrines express merely the rules of talking within the Christian community. Other communities, other rules—and no ontological claims, one way or the other."[19] Lindbeck is not finally a radical relativist. However, for reasons he never makes quite coherent, his relegating of Christian truth claims to second-order propositions sounds strangely equivocal. He actually believes that the way to ecumenical unity is through an undermining of the ontological intent of doctrine.

As a corrective to such theological-ontological relativism—which indeed might well find support among many philosophers (such as "Wittgensteinian fideists") since they have been claiming

---

19. Placher, *Unapologetic Theology*, 165–66. See Lindbeck, *Nature of Doctrine*.

this for years—Placher summarizes what he takes to be a "minimal" list of the things that "a Christian theologian needs to say."

> To summarize: (1) Christians believe that no subsequent experience will refute the essential pattern we as Christians now see in things. (2) We believe that the pattern of which Christians now catch a glimpse will ultimately be perspicuous to all. (3) Mysterious as all talk of God is, we believe that our actions in faith respond to prior acts of God, and therefore talk of God cannot be interpreted without remainder as a way of talking about human thoughts or practices.[20]

This is a promising three-article statement containing many of the basic "grammatical" rules that, indeed, ought to govern theological discourse. Add to this abstract framework a few ontologically intended illustrations so as to show how these three grammatical rules might be applied doctrinally, and we have the makings of a first-rate theological grammar. Article one (1) calls for the doctrine of the Trinity to give Christian utterance concerning the stability and steadfastness of God in his revelation coherence and point. The eschatological verification implicit in article two (2) would be groundless if did it not assume creation *ex nihilo* and the resurrection of Jesus Christ, as that resurrection is an indication of the capacity and will of God to deliver on his promise of eternal life for all. Article three (3) entails the genuine reality of the being and acts of God as the true object of human witness, together with the recognition that any valid definition of humanity lies in the realization that we are created in the image of God. Thus, the eternal God defines us before we define God or ourselves.

Few philosophers would want to grant Placher such sweeping claims on the grounds of revelation alone, which is the only basis on which such claims could conceivably be made. Knowing where Placher finally went with their insights (i.e., like Kierkegaard he broke with them), they might, as has been suggested, even feel used, or more fundamentally, ignored. Perhaps this explains why he focused less than adequately on the dehumanizing impact of

20. Placher, *Unapologetic Theology*, 166.

skepticism, nihilism, and relativism in modern culture. He is not concerned that in tying his unapologetics to pluralism the result of such a disintegrating move will be to bring his theology down. He intended all along to break with it. But if this is the case, what does his homage to worldly pluralism have to do at an intrinsic level with his theology?

There is a certain parallel between Placher's philosophic assault on Enlightenment rationalism and Emil Brunner's proposal some sixty years ago that theology should engage in a sort of negative unapologetic prolegomenon that he called "eristics." This ultimately led to Karl Barth's vociferous 1934 assault on Brunner— "No!"[21] Given what Barth had already said of Brunner's proposal, the ferocity of his "No!" should not have been a surprise.[22] Brunner had insisted that for theology to get a hearing amid the rationalistic self-confidence of the modern world, it had to engage in what Brunner called an *ad hominem* assault on the undue self-confidence of modernity. For Brunner, "Eristic theology means 'laying bare' the true character of existence by destroying the fictions of every *Weltanschauung*. But this 'laying bare' cannot be performed except by using what man can of himself know about himself."[23] Or as Karl Heim, who also took this line, saw it, "[T]here falls to Christian philosophy a merely negative task. It must 'unsecure' man."[24] The existentialism of the time seemed a particularly effective tool for such unsecuring. Barth, of course, was well aware of this, for he himself in the period of his 1922 *Epistle to the Romans* was not wholly innocent of such an eristic intent. The danger in this line, Barth had come to see, is that it permits existentialist philosophy, itself a *Weltanschauung* deeply estranged from Christianity, the first word in describing the nature of the alleged abyss of our actual existence, the implication being that existentialism provides

21. Barth and Brunner, *Natural Theology*.
22. Barth, *Church Dogmatics*, I/1, 26–33.
23. Barth and Brunner, *Natural Theology*, 114. (Barth quoting Brunner's *Zwischen den Zeiten* [1932], 529–30.)
24. Barth, *Church Dogmatics* I/1, 28.

the correct diagnosis—even if it were mistaken as to the cure. Finally, existentialism is a mere tool by which theology can bring the post-Enlightenment self-confidence of Western humanity to its knees, thereby forcing the rationalists in us to face our sin and our dependence on Christ's grace.

Suffice to say of this strategy that existential despair is not remotely the same thing as the Christian recognition of sin. Sin is a betrayal of God. It is not some free-floating anxiety that philosophers of darkness such as Heidegger (the Nazi) or Nietzsche (the Nazi saint) proclaimed to be the ultimate reality of things. Sin is discovered only when one knows the God against whom it is a betrayal, i.e., the God who has already rescued and reconciled us. Our despair is not in any sense the truth of our beings. As Barth puts it, "If Jesus Christ is the Word of Truth, the 'mirror of the fatherly heart of God' [Luther], then Nietzsche's statement that man is something to be overcome is an impudent lie."[25]

Brunner, Heim, Bultmann, and the great host of theologians whom they have influenced, ultimately, I think, prove Barth's point. Every Christian theologian who remains a Christian must break with the existential analysis of humanity's natural condition and speak of redemption in Jesus Christ as the final reality of humanity. If Jesus Christ is the last thing the theologian believes should be said, simple honesty would seem to require that Jesus Christ should also have been the first thing that should have been said. If humanity is defined by God's love, then presumably an analysis of the human situation that holds back from witnessing to the primacy of God's love (or as Barth was later to say, the very "humanity of God") until the false self-confidence of humanity can be shattered, seems to assume that humanity must be torn down before God can be praised. Without using the term "eristics," Dietrich Bonhoeffer picked up on Barth's concerns over the issues raised by an eristic, *ad hominem* strategy. "[W]e shouldn't run man down in his worldliness, but confront him with God at his strongest point, that we

25. Barth, *Humanity of God*, 51–52.

should give up all our clerical tricks, and not regard psychotherapy and existentialist philosophy as God's pioneers."[26] Bonhoeffer, who not without some justification virtually equated existentialism and psychotherapy, elsewhere waxed eloquent against the perniciousness of the existentialist and psychoanalytic undertaking.

> Of course, we now have the secularized offshoots of Christian theology, namely existentialist philosophy and the psychotherapists, who demonstrate to secure, contented, and happy mankind that it is really unhappy and desperate and simply unwilling to admit that it is in a predicament about which it knows nothing, and from which only they can rescue it. Wherever there is health, strength, security, simplicity, they scent luscious fruit to gnaw at or to lay their pernicious eggs in. They set themselves to drive people to inward despair, and then the game is in their hands. That is secularized methodism. And whom does it touch? A small number of intellectuals, of degenerates, of people who regard themselves as the most important thing in the world, and who therefore like to busy themselves with themselves. The ordinary man, who spends his everyday life at work and with his family, and of course with all kinds of diversions, is not affected. He has neither the time nor the inclination to concern himself with his existential despair, or to regard his perhaps modest share of happiness as a trial, a trouble or a calamity.[27]

Placher is no existentialist. Nevertheless, in his own more pluralistic version of "eristics," he enlists elements (albeit eclectically) of existentialism in his campaign against the self-confidence of the Enlightenment. While his assessment of the current climate is not the dark despair of post–World War I Europe—in fact, he sees the pluralism of the present climate as promising—he does not resist the temptation to use current intellectual fashions to do his theological dirty work.

If, however, one wants to criticize the Enlightenment, why not criticize it from the ground on which one actually stands, and not from some foreign base? Why not criticize it theologically?

26. Bonhoeffer, *Letters and Papers from Prison*, 346.
27. Ibid., 326–27.

The recognition that there is order in the cosmos and that its order can be penetrated by human reason is a recognition that one might even have expected to emerge from a Christendom that not only found this in the Bible, but that had Christianized those Greek philosophers (e.g., Plato, Aristotle, the Stoics) who believed in the possibility of discerning the truth. Christendom's appropriation of the Greeks proved to backfire in the Enlightenment, and the primacy of the biblical doctrine of creation gave way to a philosophic reinterpretation of creation (Deism). Thus, the Enlightenment as a religion stood in danger of elevating human rationality to the throne of God. Intent on glorifying humanity, the Enlightenment forgot that while we are created in God's image and have been granted finite dominion, our lordship does not extend to infinity; moreover, our attempts at all-inclusive rational schemas, though they are legitimate attempts insofar as they acknowledge that the cosmos is not a chaos, will always be, at best, finite and incomplete approximations of the divine "system."

However, the Enlightenment's attempt to grasp the whole scene is no more problematic than the pluralism that challenges it. If the Enlightenment can be seen as a Christian heresy, so too can the existentialism that fuels much of the postmodern absolutizing of pluralism and indeterminacy. Kierkegaard attacked the absolute human system as exemplified by Hegel. There were other earlier systems, less windy perhaps, but in their own ways all-inclusive. Kierkegaard determined not to speculate metaphysically upon final truth, but to reflect purely on that of which we could have direct knowledge, i.e., what it was to be an existent human being.

The Enlightenment produced a one-sided emphasis on, as well as an anthropocentric misreading of, the first chapter of Genesis, wherein the availability to human reason of the order and purpose of God's design was stressed together with the utter sovereignty of God, a sovereignty that Deism abstracted and distorted. Reacting against the whole line of anthropocentrism that began in the Enlightenment and continued in Hegel, Kierkegaard stressed the fragmentedness, finitude, and sin of humanity so as to underscore the pretentiousness of such pompous anthropocentricism. As such, he stressed an interpretation of existence more in line with the "J" writer's vision of creation and creation gone awry. Alas, twentieth-century existentialism employed Kierkegaard's Christian existentialist awareness of the limits of human knowledge in the service of its own nihilistic conclusions; to wit, that our existential condition reflects and alleges the nothingness that is the primal source of being. As such, existentialism is also a Christian heresy that would make the Fall the central truth that conditions all other truth and gives rise to the irreducible pluralism and disarray that must be the fruit of such babble. But to celebrate this as the desirable norm is an even greater distortion than the anthropocentric optimism of the Enlightenment. To seek an alliance with pluralism over unity hardly does justice to the biblical picture, and since Placher believes in the providential lordship of the God of Abraham, Isaac and Jacob, he finally cannot be a pluralist himself. God's unifying purpose encompasses both humanity's diversity and its disorder.

Paul shows great epistemological perception in his major treatment of the epistemological question in his first letter to the church at Corinth, Greece, by handling epistemology itself as a matter of second-order importance. Paul insists that theological knowledge is not to be placed on a par with the great Christian virtues of faith, hope, and above all love. Thus for Paul the subject of knowledge is dealt with only so that it can be forcefully put in its place as the servant of love.

> If I have prophetic powers, and understand all mysteries and all knowledge . . . but do not have love, I am nothing. . . .
>
> Love never ends. But as for prophecies, they will come to an end; as for tongues, they will cease; as for knowledge, it will come to an end. For we know only in part, and we prophesy only in part; but when the complete comes, the partial will come to an end. When I was a child, I spoke like a child, I thought like a child, I reasoned like a child; when I became an adult, I put an end to childish ways. For now we see in a

mirror, dimly, but then we will see face to face. Now I know in part; then I will know fully, even as I have been fully known. And now faith, hope, love abide, these three; and the greatest of these is love.[28]

To be sure, Paul values "knowledge or prophecy or teaching," but this is because it contributes to the praxis of love, i.e., the "upbuilding and encouragement and consolation" of the church. For these reasons, rational speech and insight are far more highly valued in the life of the church than speaking in tongues. "For those who speak in a tongue do not speak to other people but to God; for nobody understands them, since they are speaking mysteries in the Spirit."[29] While understanding or knowledge is vital to the work and life of the church, it is not an end in itself, and it cannot be so. For what we know of God is fleeting, partial, dim, childlike, and imperfect. How could such knowledge be conceived of as an ultimate end or goal?

This is not skepticism at work. It is the very opposite of skepticism. It is rather evidence of the sure and certain fact that our minds and categories cannot encompass the God who has revealed himself in Jesus Christ. And it is fully consistent with the understanding of our human grasp of revelation that dominates the Old Testament—as, for example, Moses, who is told by God, "You cannot see my face; for no one shall not see me and live."[30] He is nonetheless privileged by God to see the glory of God's passing by. Human knowledge of God in his revelation is thus radically objective, and yet it is not and cannot be direct knowledge.

The distinction that Karl Barth draws between the primary and secondary objectivity of God is illuminating. Barth recognizes that "inevitably" to speak of God at all is to "ascribe objectivity to God." This must be true because God, who in his eternal being loves in freedom, "certainly knows Himself first of all, God is

28. 1 Cor 13:2, 8ff.
29. 1 Cor 14:2–3, 6.
30. Exod 33:20.

first and foremost objective to Himself. . . . In His triune life as such, objectivity, and with it knowledge, is divine reality before creaturely objectivity and knowledge exist."[31] What distinguishes this primary objectivity of God to himself from the secondary objectivity of God for us in his revelation is not any diminution of truth. The secondary objectivity of God is the truth of God, but in a particular form "suitable to us, the creature."[32] Thus, while truly present, he comes to us "clothed under the sign and veil of other objects different from himself."[33]

Barth sees this distinction not merely as a formal epistemological one, but a distinction that defines the nature of Christian faith and trust in the reliability of God in his standing behind the promises revealed in his works or acts.

> At bottom, knowledge of God in faith is always this indirect knowledge of God, knowledge of God in His works, and in these particular works—in the determining and using of certain creaturely realities to bear witness to the divine objectivity. What distinguishes faith from unbelief, erroneous faith and superstition is that it is content with this indirect knowledge of God. It does not think that the knowledge of God in His works is insufficient. On the contrary, it is grateful really to know the real God in His works. It really lets itself be shown the objectivity of God by their objectivity. But it also holds fast to the particularity of these works. It does not arbitrarily choose objects to set up as signs, in that way inventing a knowledge of God at its own good-pleasure. It knows God by means of the objects chosen by God Himself.[34]

Barth puts this somewhat paradoxically: "We really know Him in His objectivity (even if it is clothed); and we really know Him only His clothed objectivity."[35] It might be stated even more paradoxically. God always reveals himself through that which he is not. He

31. Barth, *Church Dogmatics* II/1, 16.
32. Ibid.
33. Ibid.
34. Ibid., 16–17.
35. Ibid., 16.

is not a wind at the sea of reeds. He is not the invasion of Israel by Assyria. He is not the human flesh of Jesus. But in all these he has been revealed. However, the fact that our knowledge of God must be described in term of such a paradoxical dialectic does not in any sense open Christian theology to the notion that because our revelatory knowledge of God has this secondary quality it is equivocal (Tillich) or it can be contradicted by some deeper hidden intention (Luther).

Barth explicitly rejects anything like the Tillichian doctrine of symbolic knowledge and the notion that our knowledge of God is less than objective—"the door is shut against any non-objective knowledge of God"[36]—since God is objective to himself and God's secondary objectivity for and unto us "is fully true, for it has correspondence and basis in His primary objectivity."[37] This beckons epistemology to quit its palace and set up shop nearer to the indirect and paradoxical acts of God in history.

36. Ibid.
37. Ibid.

Epilogue

AT THE close of chapter three the question was raised as to whether, given the fact that we are children of our culture, a radical, anti-apologetic fideism can ever be fully coherent. Without disputing the fact that Christianity is grounded in God's self-disclosure, we can never ignore that God's self-disclosure comes to us in our historical, personal situation, and thus we hear God's words with ears attuned not to the first century and certainly not to heaven, but to our own time. However, beyond and above such considerations, a lofty disregard for the apologetic implications of the modern epistemological crisis suggests an attitude that would seem to stand at odds with the universal saving power of the cross; indeed, an attitude that would fail fully to grasp that logic of faith in the unlimited atoning significance of the death of Jesus Christ that compels Christianity to stand in solidarity with the world in its sin and in its doubt.

Radical, anti-apologetic fideism inevitably carries the suggestion of a we/they vision of the world. To wit, there are the believers who believe because they have been granted sight by a miracle of the Holy Spirit, and there are unbelievers who doubt because in the Holy Spirit's freedom they have been kept in the dark. In this context, we are once again reminded of Augustine's extension of his doctrine of double predestination into the realm of ethics: for Augustine, because the ancient pagan virtues were merely the ideals of a finally blind unbelief, the pagan's "virtuous" acts, however splendid, must finally be seen as "splendid vices."[1]

---

1. On Augustine's use of this phrase, see above, chapter 5, footnote 2.

One need not, however, resort to double predestination to account for the brokenness of human culture. One could simply declare the total depravity of all things human, pivot 180 degrees, and then claim that finally all will be saved through Christ's atoning work. However, such thinking finally places any universalist Christian hope so out of phase with its dark appraisal of the whole of human culture, so much an utterly *ad hoc* divine add-on, that though such a surprise happy ending may not strictly speaking be illogical, it nevertheless tends to die the death of its own arbitrariness.

Our contemporary situation makes this problem particularly acute if our philosophic and theological doubts are finally reduced to mere indications of human blindness and alienation. Given such thinking it is difficult to escape the implication that our whole culture must thereby be judged as having been built on sin, with very little "splendid" about its vice, for it is clear that our culture is fueled by a drastic and hostile secular spirit. Yet the West has parlayed its rationalism, pluralistic skepticism, even its cynicism, into the richest, most glitteringly powerful civilization history has as yet known.

Of course, we have witnessed much evil as a result of that power: ruinous wars, environmental and ecological destruction, the poor getting poorer as the rich get richer, and so on. Nevertheless, such power has the potential for positively affecting the quality of human life as well, as we who are the beneficiaries of technology, availing ourselves as we do of technology's wonders, can attest. We are all too deeply acculturated to turn our backs on culture, however, and insofar as Christians we attempt to do so we surrender the very means by which to transform the culture that may indeed be conformed in some small way to the love of Jesus Christ.

If Christians finally resolve those tensions related to being *in* the world by a mere grudging acceptance of the givenness of the world, this sullen reticence has curious consequences for our Christian witness, not the least of which is that "Christian" disdain for our profane culture oddly skews the whole Christian claim of God's love, leaving us with the odd formula: God so loves the world, but so hates the world's accomplishments.

Further, can we, with straight faces, luxuriate in the rich offerings of the world; that is, transport ourselves nearly anywhere on the globe, acquire goods, services, and information of every imaginable type at the click of a mouse, access state-of-the-art medical care, eat whatever we want whenever we want, partake of any form of entertainment that compels us, deny ourselves no creature comfort, and then turn around and claim that all of this is merely the product of sin?

And not just our own culture would have to stand so accused. Has there been any other culture qualitatively better, i.e., more godly? Ancient Israel? The prophets hardly thought so. Ancient Rome, Greece, or Egypt? Modern Israel? Modern Palestine? Every culture comes under judgment. There is and has been no kingdom of God on earth. Yet, does such a quite proper acknowledgment of inevitable historical imperfection entail a concomitant rejection of all things human, so that God is ultimately represented as loving only what *he* makes, while hating what we contribute to creation? As if the whole of biblical theology comes to focus in the story of the Tower of Babel?

Such thinking cannot help but imply that God's love is less agapic and rather more narcissistic, as God is represented as loving us only as we are mirrors of himself. The more Christianity is suspicious of the human genius that makes for culture, the more God's universal love is made incomprehensible, as God's love is represented as loving nothing we ever actually are and do but only an ideal of what we might in theory have been and done but to which we could never in practice attain.

It is far better to read the epistemological turmoil of contemporary culture and theology's obligation to take an apologetic stance toward it in the light, once again, of Augustine's confessional prayer: "Oh God, our hearts are restless until they find their rest in thee."[2] The epistemological crisis of the contemporary world is but

2. *Confessions* 1.1.2. This Augustine is a rather different Augustine than

a symptom of the contemporary world's paradoxically confident yet brokenhearted, hopeful yet despairing quest for God. The human being *is* a believing animal. We cannot even doubt without grounding our doubt in some sort of belief.

Traditional apologetic theologies of either an orthodox or a liberal stripe have generally made the wrong thing of the fact that while all human beings must have beliefs to live by, many have not found the one true God. Though orthodoxy and liberalism approach this dilemma very differently, they both assume that what is needed to breach the cleavage between God and ourselves is strong and sophisticated argumentation. However, we must finally ask: Does not the very power of such argumentation finally turn Christianity, the religion rooted in the crucified and rejected "King of the Jews," into a religion of deeply imperialistic pretentiousness?

Apologetic theology has too long presumed to be able either to imperiously "prove" the existence of God (orthodox apologetics) or to correlate the questions implicit in all culture with the Christian answer so as to prove that all culture leads to Christ—thus attempting imperialistically to co-op culture (liberal apologetics). Rather, the apologetic crisis occasioned by the world's unbelief ought to be the signal for Christians, in the name of Jesus Christ's sacrificial solidarity with those who rejected him (keeping in mind that we remain among them), out of sympathy for unbelief, to seek solidarity with those whose rejection takes the form of unbelief.

Such solidarity grows above all out of Christ's sacrificial solidarity with us. However, it also commends itself as we examine our own experience of faith, and thus is not unrelated to the matter of theological epistemology. Knowing, as we must, that faith has come to us as an undeserved and virtually irresistible gift, are we not thereby compelled to testify in solidarity with the world and consistent with our own experience that unbelief is not, first of all, due to recalcitrant sinfulness or to some stubborn philosophical

---

the later, dualistically predestinarian Augustine who would condemn all non-Christian or pre-Christian sentiment as splendid vice.

unwillingness to believe? The root cause of the world's rejection lies elsewhere: in the fact that the church has failed to make belief in Jesus Christ a patent reality; and above all in the patent fact of much contemporary experience that God himself has kept his own silence.

God has permitted the church's pitiful witness to remain Jesus Christ's prime witness to the world, and even when the church strives to be faithful, God so often chooses to remain in eclipse. Is it any wonder that unbelievers and even believers find little earthly recourse than to strike out on their own in order to find beliefs or systematized doubts to live by? We are believing animals. If we cannot believe in God, we must believe in something. If humanity's worldly quest begins in God's silence, is it any wonder that it finds answers that presuppose the absence of God? No argument, no word we can speak can drown out the silence of a God who remained silent even when his Son cried out for a word of assurance from the cross.

The church, in faithfulness to the word of God it *has* heard, cannot finally affirm godless beliefs that arise out of the plurality of the world, however rational, extra-rational, ethical, modern, postmodern, they may be. So called "theological atheism" is a jaded mockery of the living God. Nevertheless, when the church is compelled to say "no" to the world, its situation is so oddly paradoxical as to lead to an almost numbing circumspection. For in the very act of saying "no" to the radical doubt and despair of one's fellow human beings, it is forced to call to mind the epistemological foundation on which it has come to claim to know God and thus why doubt, despair, and skepticism are in the final analysis, simply a mistake.

This foundation is, of course, the resurrection of Jesus Christ, the event in which God has made his power and love manifest. Yet obviously the resurrection cannot be viewed in isolation. Christ's resurrection is the fruit of his self-sacrificing passion, a passion in which he himself was brought to the point of radical questioning, not only concerning his very being as God's Son, but concerning

God's perfect faithfulness as well. When Jesus from the cross demanded to know, "My God, my God, why have you forsaken me?"—he was met with silence.[3]

Thus, when doubters doubt God, are they not recapitulating in their own experience a crucial element of the passion of Jesus Christ? How can we deny that there is in Jesus Christ's cry from the cross a certain epistemological estrangement of the Son from the Father? I am not suggesting that doubt is as adequate a response to Jesus Christ as is faith. This would be an absurdity. But only barely so. Recognizing the knife edge between faith and unfaith, and how arbitrary it is from our point of view (the only point of view we *can* adopt) that we believe in Jesus Christ's universal love and our neighbor does not, we have no right, in Jesus' name, to stand *for* God's truth by standing *against* the world in its doubt. The "for-or-against" model of human relations can no longer be countenanced in the name of the church or any other name.

God has entered the world to achieve atonement of and with the world, but ironically in many ways the *epistemological* problem is exacerbated by his coming. For God came not in manifest power, but in the weakness of the suffering servant. Christ comes in a way that allows him even in the mightiest of his mighty works to be seen variously; that is, in his own time he was accused of being possessed of a demon and being a false prophet. Our contemporary approach is to claim there are no miracles; thus, stories of his mighty works must be explained in naturalistic terms, or in terms of the alleged superstitions of the pre-modern evangelists. Yet even when Jesus Christ's glory was manifested in his resurrection, it was a glory that only a few witnessed—he didn't appear to everyone—and even those who did see him were left intellectually dislocated and strained for explanations. Today the resurrection proclaimed in our mainline churches is so qualified by explanations and provisos that it might seem doubtful whether the churches are talking about the original event.

---

3. Matt 27:46; Mark 15:34.

Nevertheless, our doctrinal and epistemological disarray notwithstanding, how is it that Christians, despite their disagreements on such decisive questions as Christ's divinity, his atoning death, and his resurrection, are drawn to him while non-Christians are not? This, moreover, is to say nothing of the problems that the very existence of non-Christian religions creates for questions such as revelation or the possibility of religious "truth." Even if it proves true that God was indeed in Jesus Christ, even if it could definitively be shown that Christian faith is not mere delusion, until its truth becomes manifest and is grasped in a manner that makes it knowable by all, Jesus Christ's coming offers no universal, epistemological solution, but only a further complication of modern epistemological confusion.

Thus, the example of Jesus Christ urges us toward solidarity, yet conversely the very badge of Jesus Christ that we wear singles us out from non-Christian humanity. If we attempt to overcome the inevitable distance—if not alienation—that faith creates between ourselves as Christians and unbelievers by compelling apologetic arguments, such argumentation seems to run counter to the humility of Christ who made no argument by which to defend himself—"But he was silent and did not answer."[4] On the other hand, Jesus did not take silent refuge in a systematically closed fideism. His was a "fideism" of a different sort.

On the basis of what can be surmised from Mark's account, had Jesus persisted in silence throughout his trial before the Sanhedrin, perhaps he might have escaped the cross. His accusers could not agree.[5] Thus, presumably, the case was weak. However, while Jesus would not engage in even a personal and certainly not a theological apologetic, he did, when it was demanded of him, testify and thereby deliver himself up to death. When pushed by the high priest, "Are you the Messiah, the Son of the Blessed One?" Jesus could not remain true to his calling and remain silent. "'I am; and 'you will see the Son of Man seated at the right hand of Power,'

---

4. Mark 14:61; cf. Matt 26:63.
5. Mark 14:56; cf. Matt 26:59f.

and 'coming with the clouds of heaven.'" At this, "the high priest tore his clothes and said, 'Why do we still need witnesses? You have heard his blasphemy!'"[6]

Jesus made his startlingly imperious claim knowing he had sealed his fate unless perchance his accusers found in his own fideist utterance the occasion of their own transformation. However, judged by how imperfectly even his disciples had grasped his claim, Jesus must have known of a certainty what would result from his confession. Jesus' fideist assertion supported by nothing save his person and ministry did not provide him a defensive fortress that the critics of this world could not breach. It was a fideism that made him radically vulnerable. Was it not perhaps his "right" to give such fideist offense, in that he was willing to incur in his own being the wrath he incited? If his utterance gave the high priest anguish, Jesus was willing to stand in solidarity with that anguish, by bearing the far greater anguish of crucifixion. Might there be some basic principle in this for apologetic theology? Might it be that it must first and foremost take a fideist stance and then demonstrate that stance in self-sacrificial solidarity with unbelievers? But this is nothing more than Dietrich Bonhoeffer knew, following the apostle Paul: "It is not abstract argument, but example, that gives its [the church's] word emphasis and power."[7]

Perhaps theology has sinned away its right to be apologetic. Its pristine emphasis on method, its flirtations with atheism, its substitution of the mores of academia for Christian rectitude, have made it a wonderment even to the few in the pews who give it any thought at all. But it also generally plays virtually no part in the calculations of the elite of the intellectual and scientific communities, who regard theology with a disdainful sneer. Why would anyone listen to us theologians? We are experts in areas that might suggest that we could have some special knowledge about ultimate matters. But there is nothing special in our lives. Our arguments

---

6. Mark 14:61–64; Matt 26:63–66; Luke 22:67–71.
7. Bonhoeffer, *Letters and Papers from Prison*, 383. See 1 Cor 2.4; 4:20.

are rendered curiously hollow when it seems apparent that we who are the masters of such arguments have not ourselves been transformed by them.

We have more to prove to the world than any argument could ever establish. In the last analysis, the true apologetic theology is followed by a life lived in such a manner that people will press upon one to inquire as to what lies behind such a life. Were the church and its theologians to live lives that showed some of the fruits of the Spirit—"love, joy, peace, patience, kindness, goodness, faithfulness, gentleness, self-control"[8]—the world might actually give them heed.

---

8. Gal 5:22b–3a.

Bibliography

Altizer, Thomas J. J. *The Gospel of Christian Atheism*. Philadelphia: Westminster, 1966.

Aquinas, Thomas. *Summa Theologica: Complete English Edition in Five Volumes*. Translated by the Fathers of the English Dominican Province. Westminster, MD: Christian Classics, 1948.

Augustine. *The City of God against the Pagans*. Translated by R. W. Dyson. Cambridge Texts in the History of Political Thought. Cambridge: Cambridge University Press, 1998.

———. *Saint Augustine's Confessions*. Translated by Henry Chadwick. New York: Oxford University Press, 1991.

———. *On Christian Teaching*. Translated and edited by R. P. H. Green. New York: Oxford University Press, 1997.

———. *The Trinity*. Translated by Edmund Hill, OP. Edited by John Rotelle, OSA. New York: New City, 1991.

Barth, Karl. *Church Dogmatics I/1, The Doctrine of the Word of God*. Translated by G. T. Thompson. Edinburgh: T. & T. Clark, 1936.

———. *Church Dogmatics II/1, The Doctrine of God*. Translated by T. H. L. Parker. Edited by G. W. Bromiley and T. F. Torrance. Edinburgh: T. & T. Clark, 1957.

———. *Church Dogmatics III/4, The Doctrine of Creation*. Translated by A. T. Mackay. Edinburgh: T. & T. Clark, 1961.

———. *Church Dogmatics IV/2, The Doctrine of Reconciliation*. Translated by G. W. Bromiley. Edited by G. W. Bromiley and T. F. Torrance. Edinburgh: T. & T. Clark, 1958.

———. *The Epistle to the Romans*. 6th ed. Translated by Edward C. Hoskyns. Oxford: Oxford University Press, 1968.

———. *The Humanity of God*. Translated by John Newton Thomas and Thomas Wieser. Richmond, VA: Knox, 1960.

Barth, Karl, and Emil Brunner. *Natural Theology: Comprising "Nature and Grace" by Professor Dr. Emil Brunner and the Reply "No" by Dr. Karl Barth*. Translated by Peter Fraenkel. London: Centenary, 1946.

Bartsch, Hans Werner, editor. *Kerygma and Myth: A Theological Debate.* 2 vols. Translated by Reginald H. Fuller. London: SPCK, 1962, 1964.

Bettenson, Henry, editor. *Documents of the Christian Church.* 2nd ed. Oxford: Oxford University Press, 1967.

Bonhoeffer, Dietrich. *Letters and Papers from Prison.* Edited by Eberhard Bethge. New York: Macmillan, 1971.

Bultmann, Rudolf. "Bultmann Replies to His Critics," "The Case for Demythologizing: A Reply," and "New Testament and Mythology." In *Kerygma and Myth: A Theological Debate,* 2 vols., edited by Hans Wernder Bartsch, 2:191–94. Translated by Reginald H. Fuller. London: SPCK, 1962.

———. *Existence and Faith: The Shorter Writings of Rudolf Bultmann.* Translated and edited by Schubert M. Ogden. New York: Meridian, 1960.

Feuerbach, Ludwig. *The Essence of Christianity.* 3rd ed. Edited and translated by Marian Evans. The English and Foreign Philosophical Library 15. London: Trübner, 1881.

Goetz, Ronald. "Process Theology Debate Continues." *Christian Century* (March 4, 1987) 224–25.

Gunton, Colin. *Becoming and Being: The Doctrine of God in Charles Hartshorne and Karl Barth.* Oxford: Oxford University Press, 1978.

Gustafson, James. *Ethics from a Theocentric Perspective.* Vol. 1, *Theology and Ethics.* Chicago: University of Chicago Press, 1981.

Hawking, Stephen W. *A Short History of Time: From the Big Bang to Black Holes.* New York: Bantam, 1988.

Hick, John. *An Interpretation of Religion: Human Responses to the Transcendent.* 2nd ed. New Haven, CT: Yale University Press, 2004.

———. *Metaphor of God Incarnate: Christology in a Pluralistic Age.* 2nd ed. Louisville: Knox, 2005.

Hume, David. "Dialogues Concerning Natural Religion." In *David Hume Dialogues and Natural History of Religion,* edited by J. C. A. Gaskin, 134–85. Oxford World Classics. Oxford: Oxford University Press, 1993.

Jaspers, Karl. "Myth and Religion." In *Kerygma and Myth: A Theological Debate,* vol. 1. Second edition. Edited by Hans Werner Bartsch. Translated by Reginald H. Fuller. London: SPCK, 1964.

Jenson, Robert W. *God According to the Gospel: The Triune Identity.* Philadelphia: Fortress, 1982.

———. *Systematic Theology: The Triune God.* Vol. 1. New York and Oxford: Oxford University Press, 1997.

Kaufman, Gordon. *God the Problem.* Cambridge, MA: Harvard University Press, 1972.

———. *The Theological Imagnination.* Philadelphia: Westminster, 1981.

———. *Theology for a Nuclear Age.* Philadelphia: Westminster, 1985.

Kierkegaard, Soren. *Concluding Unscientific Postscript.* Translated by David F. Swenson and Walter Lowrie. Princeton: Princeton University Press, 1941.

———. *A Kierkegaard Anthology.* Edited by Robert Bretall. The Modern Library. New York: Random, 1946.

———. *On Authority and Revelation.* Translated, edited, and with an introduction by Walter Lowrie. Princeton: Princeton University Press, 1955.

Lindbeck, George. *The Nature of Doctrine.* Philadelphia: Westminster, 1984.

Mascall, E. L. *Existence and Analogy: A Sequel to "He Who Is."* N.p.: Archon, 1967.

McFague, Sally. *Models of God: Theology for an Ecological, Nuclear Age.* Philadelphia: Fortress, 1987.

Mozley, J. K. *The Doctrine of the Atonement.* Studies in Theology. New York: Scribner's, 1916.

Placher, William. *Unapologetic Theology: A Christian Voice in Pluralistic Conversation* Louisville: Knox, 1989.

Raschke, Carl A. "The Deconstruction of God." In *Deconstruction and Theology*, by Thomas J. J., Altizer et al., 7–8. New York: Crossroad, 1982.

Robinson, John A. T. *Honest to God.* Philadelphia: Westminster, 1963.

Rowe, William L. *Religious Symbols and God: A Philosophical Study of Tillich's Theology.* Chicago and London: University of Chicago Press, 1968.

Smart, James D. *The Divided Mind of Modern Theology: Karl Barth and Rudolf Bultmann, 1908-1933.* Philadelphia: Westminster, 1967.

Schmithals, Walter. *An Introduction to the Theology of Rudolf Bultmann.* Minneapolis: Augsburg, 1967.

Smith, Dwight Moody. "The Historical Jesus in Paul Tillich's Theology." *Journal of Religion* 46 (1966) 144.

Stout, Jeffrey. *Ethics After Babel.* Boston: Beacon, 1988.

Taylor, Mark C. *Erring: A Post Modern A/theology.* Chicago: University of Chicago Press, 1984.

Thistlethwaite, Susan. *A Shuddering Dawn: Religious Studies and the Nuclear Age.* Edited by Ira Chernus and Edward T. Linenthal. New York: State University of New York Press, 1989.

Tillich, Hannah. *From Time to Time.* New York: Stein & Day, 1973.

Tillich, Paul. *Dynamics of Faith.* New York: Harper & Row, 1957.

———. *On the Boundary: An Autobiographical Sketch.* New York: Scribner's, 1966.

———. *Systematic Theology.* 2 vols. Chicago: University of Chicago Press, 1951–57.

von Balthasar, Hans Urs. *The Theology of Karl Barth.* Translated by John Drury. New York, et al.: Holt, Rinehardt, & Winston, 1971.

Vulgamore, Melvin L. "Tillich's Erotic Solution." *Encounter* 45 (1984) 193–212.

Wetzel, James. "Splendid Vice and Secular Virtues: Variations on Milbank's Augustine." *The Journal of Religious Ethics* 32 (2004) 272–300.

Wheat, Leonard F. *Paul Tillich's Dialectical Humanism: Unmasking the God Above God.* Baltimore, MD: Hopkins, 1970.

Whitehead, Alfred North. *The Principle of Relativity with Applications to Physical Science.* Cambridge: Cambridge at the University Press, 1922.

www.ingramcontent.com/pod-product-compliance
Lightning Source LLC
Chambersburg PA
CBHW070907160426
43193CB00011B/1393